Hiking
Utah's
Summits

by
Paula Huff and Tom Wharton

FALCON®
HELENA, MONTANA

A FALCON GUIDE

Falcon Publishing is continually expanding its list of recreational guidebooks. All books include detailed descriptions, accurate maps, and all the information necessary for enjoyable trips. You can order extra copies of this book and get information and prices for other Falcon guidebooks by writing Falcon, P.O. Box 1718, Helena, MT 59624 or calling toll-free 1-800-582-2665. Also, please ask for a free copy of our current catalog. Visit our Web site at http:\\www.falconguide.com

Printed in Canada.

10 9 8 7 6 5 4 3 2 1

All black-and-white photos by author.

Cover photo by Rod Millar

Library of Congress Cataloging-in-Publication Data
Huff, Paula.
    Hiking Utah's summits / by Paula Huff and Tom Wharton.
        p.   cm
    Includes bibliographical references (p.).
    ISBN 1-56044-588-2 (pbk.)
    1. Hiking—Utah—Guidebooks.   2. Mountaineering—Utah—Guidebooks.   2. Utah—Guidebooks.   4. Utah—History.   I. Wharton, Tom, 1950-   .   II. Title.
GV199.42U8H84   1997
917.9204'33--dc21   91-14946
                                                                                CIP

CAUTION

Outdoor recreational activities are by their very nature potentially hazardous. All participants in such activities must assume the responsibility for their own actions and safety. The information contained in this guidebook cannot replace sound judgment and good decision–making skills, which help reduce risk exposure, nor does the scope of this book allow for disclosure of all the potential hazards and risks involved in such activities.

Learn as much as possible about the outdoor recreational activities in which you participate, prepare for the unexpected, and be cautious. The reward will be a safer and more enjoyable experience.

 Text pages printed on recycled paper.

*To all my friends and relatives who
patiently waited for me at the top*
    —*Tom Wharton*

*To Stephen Hunt, whose love for the
outdoors is infectious*
    — *Paula Huff*

CONTENTS

PREFACE

Outdoor enthusiasts are collectors.

Some collect snapshots of the beautiful places they visit. Others gather memories of friends and families. A few remember places by purchasing a souvenir or keeping a rock.

To an increasing degree, many hikers pride themselves on bagging peaks. A club in Colorado, for example, boasts members who climb 14,000-foot mountains. Another national group is made up of folks determined to climb the highest point in all 50 states.

Thus, when *Salt Lake Tribune* staff writer Paula Huff approached me with the idea of writing a series of stories on climbing to the highest peak in each of Utah's 29 counties for the newspaper's weekly recreation page which I edit, I was intrigued. She said this would be one way that our newspaper could celebrate Utah's 1996 statehood centennial year with its readers.

Our section has been a part of three major series since 1991, all of which proved popular with readers. One examined the natural history of the Great Salt Lake. Another looked at issues involving the canyons east of the Wasatch Front. The third chronicled the history of wildlife management in Utah.

Collecting each of the highest peaks in our state would become the fourth major series of the 1990s to appear in *The Salt Lake Tribune* recreation section. It would take Paula and I 18 months to complete. Her vision was not to simply write a series of where-to-hike stories, but to compile an in-depth article on each of the tallest peaks. The stories would include not only information on the difficulty of the hike and how to reach the summit, but details on how the peak got its name, its geology and its human history.

Since peaks were shared in several counties and some peaks were located in close proximity to one another, the series consisted of 24 separate stories. Many hikers from around Utah tried to collect the articles and wondered if the series would be repeated. What follows in this book is a compilation of those stories which also include trail maps, something not in the original *Salt Lake Tribune* series.

Part of the fun of the series came when we discovered that three of the highest points were unnamed. With help from readers, the Utah Committee for Geographic Names, the U.S. Geological Survey and the Utah Geological Survey, the *Tribune* proposed names for the highest peaks in Rich, Kane and Wasatch counties. Those monikers should be made official by the end of 1997.

While Paula Huff did not write every story in the series, she climbed every peak. She left me some of the easier expeditions while she tackled the more difficult hiking challenges.

We had help from plenty of "friends" in completing the project. Winford C. Bludworth, Salt Lake City, and Paul Hatch, Kaysville, researched the location of the highest peak in each county. Geologists from the Utah Geological Survey and former state geologist Genevieve Atwood donated their time and expertise. The staff at the Utah Historical Society provided often difficult-to-find human history of some of the mountains. Steve Lewis, a passionate Utah hiker, photographer, and back country skier, served as a guide. *Tribune* artist Steve Baker compiled many of the graphics in the book. *Tribune* outdoor writer Craig Hansell contributed input into the series as well. District rangers at the USDA Forest Service and Bureau of Land Management were always helpful.

When hiking to these peaks, be aware that many do not involve crossing private land. However, when it is necessary to do so, be respectful by asking first. As is the case with all hikes, hikers should go into the backcountry prepared with a good set of boots, plenty of water, and a pack full of basic emergency gear such as matches, first aid kits, and duct tape, Paula Huff's all-purpose fix-all. Try to tread lightly on the land and pick up all the litter you see on the way to the top.

Hiking to the highest peak in all 29 Utah counties is a worthy and ambitious goal, especially for those of us who enjoy collecting outdoor memories.

Tom Wharton
Recreation Editor
The Salt Lake Tribune

LOCATOR MAP

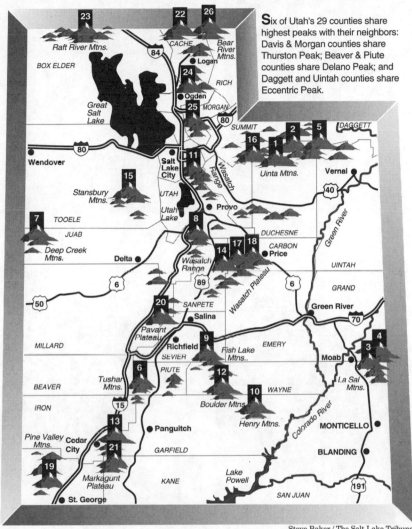

Six of Utah's 29 counties share highest peaks with their neighbors: Davis & Morgan counties share Thurston Peak; Beaver & Piute counties share Delano Peak; and Daggett and Uintah counties share Eccentric Peak.

Steve Baker / The Salt Lake Tribune

Listed in order of elevation

1 Kings Peak
13,528 ft.

2 Gilbert Peak
13,442 ft.

3 Mt. Peale
12,721 ft.

4 Mt. Waas
12,331 ft.

5 Eccentric Peak
12,276 ft.

6 Delano Peak
12,169 ft.

7 Ibapah Peak
12,087 ft.

8 Mt. Nebo
north peak
11,928 ft.

9 Fish Lake
Hightop
11,633 ft.

10 Mt. Ellen
11,522 ft.

11 American Fork
Twin Peaks
11,489 ft.

12 Bluebell Knoll
11,320 ft.

13 Brian Head Peak
11,307 ft.

14 South Tent
Mountain
11,285 ft.

15 Deseret Peak
11,031 ft.

16 Unnamed Peak
proposed name
Mt. Cardwell
10,743 ft.

17 East Mountain
10,743 ft.

18 Monument Peak
10,452 ft.

19 Signal Peak
10,365 ft.

20 Mine Camp Peak
10,222 ft.

21 Unnamed Peak
proposed name
Andy Nelson Peak
10,027 ft.

22 Naomi Peak
9,979 Ft.

23 Bull Mountain
9,920 ft.

24 Willard Peak
9,764 ft.

25 Thurston
Peak 9,707 ft.

26 Unnamed Peak
proposed name
Bridger Peak
9,255 ft.

The hike to the north peak of Mt. Nebo is steep and precarious in spots, but the views make the hike worthwhile. Paula Huff

INTRODUCTION

Say "Utah," and the picture that pops into mind is high deserts, deep canyons and scattered mountain ranges. Peaks don't often dominate the frame. But Utah is actually the rooftop of the United States.

According to the Highpointers, a nationwide hiking club, average elevation of the tallest peaks in each county statewide is 11,222 feet above sea level. The tallest peaks in Colorado's counties give it a second-place ranking, at 10,791 feet, followed by Nevada, 10,764 feet, and Wyoming, 10,179 feet. Alaska—home of Mount McKinley, North America's highest mountaintop at 20,320 feet—is sixth. Its state average elevation of county peaks is 9,280 feet. Nearly every Utah town sits in the shadow of a snow-clad peak begging to be climbed. These hills have stories to tell.

American Indians drove big game over cliffs in the Uintas. Mormon pioneers hauled knot-free logs from the Pine Valley Mountains near St. George to make pipes for the organ at Temple Square. On vertical rock faces near Ogden, miners blasted boulders and built mason walls to make trails for donkey trains leading to underground ore.

In the early part of this century, "society girls" shocked Utah by hiking tough trails in the Wasatch—while wearing pants. Today, urbanites of both genders escape the press of business in mountain meadows statewide.

Harold Goodro has been doing it 70 years. And—in spite of the fact that he carries a 20-pound oxygen tank to breathe—79-year-old Goodro has no intentions of stopping.

"I'll probably drop dead by a stream side," he says while inching up a trail in Big Cottonwood Canyon, an English driving cap holding down his stiff, white hair. "I've dedicated my life to getting out and tromping around and exploring."

A Sporting Goods Manufacturers Association survey says Utah and Idaho have the highest percentage of hikers per capita in the United States. But Goodro, a 50-year member of the Wasatch Mountain Club, believes the state's recent immigrants scramble up mountains more often than second- and third-generation Utahns.

It seems like newcomers have always been captivated by the peaks. Take the story of John Brown, who was among a group of four pioneers to explore the tallest peak overlooking the Salt Lake Valley less than a month after the Mormons arrived.

It took one day to ride horses to the foothills. At 8 A.M. on August 21, 1847, they began to walk up the face of Broads Fork Twin Peaks. They traveled light—carrying no food, guns, coats or bedrolls. Eight hours later, Brown's journal explains, they ascended the west peak of Twin Peaks. "One man gave out and lay down by a snow bank," Brown writes. He determined the elevation was 11,219 feet above sea level and that the temperature was 55 degrees at 5 P.M. Exhausted, they started down the mountain. They were miles from camp when night fell.

"Being very dark, we got separated in climbing over the rocks," Brown writes. "We had to feel our way lest we fall over a precipice. At 10 o'clock, Brother (Albert) Carrington and myself lay down under a scrubby tree. Being so tired we could not proceed, and not knowing where either of the other men were, we found a place between the rocks large enough to lie down and not in a horizontal position, but at an angle of about 45 degrees."

At 5 A.M., Carrington and Brown rose, "being somewhat rested, yet very sore," and continued down the mountain without having neither "supper, dinner or breakfast." After walking 1½ miles they found William Rust, who was "given out."

"We being in the same fix could not assist him," Brown writes. "We reached camp at 7:30 A.M., where we found our other companion, Brother Wilson ...who had made his way through the night. We then returned to the city, satisfied with our first attempt at climbing mountains."

Brown's was the first written account, but American Indians roamed Utah's mountains before white settlers had ever heard of this place, says David Madsen, state archaeologist.

Long straight rows of stones that lead to cliffs give clues to hunts throughout the state, Madsen says. Brush was propped on top of these rocks. And mountain sheep and elk were funneled into the shoots and forced over the brink. Hunting blinds can still be found, too.

"But there isn't any evidence these people hiked for pleasure," Madsen adds. "Hike is a strange term because what they were doing was part of their livelihood. They didn't separate their life into work and recreation. It was a mix. I'm sure they were in the mountains for spiritual reasons as well."

Brigham Young also was inspired by the Wasatch. Millwright Frederick Kesler twice escorted Brigham Young to see "beautiful lakes" in Big Cottonwood Canyon, says Charles Keller, an author writing a history of the Wasatch. "When Brigham Young came home he sent out invitations to the ninth festival celebrating the Mormons entering the valley. It was held at those lakes."

Now known as the lakes near Brighton, some 450 Salt Lakers showed up for the 1857 "picnic party" in 71 carriages and wagons hauled by 291 horses and mules.

By the 1880s, interest in the canyons had exploded among the affluent. Artists like Alfred Lambourne, Henry Culmer, Charles R. Savage, and George Martin Ottinger were traipsing the hills to make sketches and write articles for newspapers and magazines.

Salt Lakers could take the Utah Southern Railroad to Sandy, then catch the Wasatch and Jordan Valley Railroad to the mouth of Little Cottonwood Canyon. Along narrow-gauge tracks, mules pulled buggies packed with people to Alta.

"It took two days to get to Brighton, but people could suddenly afford to take the time and go there," Keller notes.

Women were no foreigners to these adventures. A female teacher who "held to the abhorrence of men" decided to hike alone to Bald Mountain near Park City, a writer with the pseudonym Amalric writes in an 1881 magazine called *Contributor*. She "strapped a long-necked bottle of strong tea to her shoulders, and with staff in hand, proceeded upon her journey.... Her soul was charmed to the sublimity of nature."

Senators, supreme court judges, and a defeated candidate for president had asked her hand in marriage, but she fell in love with a miner she met on her hike and married.

After the turn of the century, health was the driving force behind mountain trips, says Alexis Kelner, an outdoor author who lives in Salt Lake City. "Everything was coal heated around that time and the cities were dirty." Kelner says. "So you can understand why an outdoor clean-air movement was started."

High schools organized hiking clubs. Separate University of Utah mens' and womens' groups began tramping. And in 1913, people who had met in the mountains began walking together. On May 13, 1920, these friends incorporated. They became the Wasatch Mountain Club.

"Men only" was the club's refrain in the beginning, until sisters and girlfriends of the original 13 members pleaded to go along. After being told "not to be a nuisance and to carry their own baggage," women were allowed, Lawrence Vanderplas writes in his 1974 history of the club.

"Women in those days were never seen wearing pants; this was considered immoral," Vanderplas says. "But for girls to be wearing long skirts in the presence of men on mountain climbing expeditions was neither practical nor modest. Ignoring much criticism from church authorities, some young women were courageous enough in about 1916 to start a new tradition in this area: wearing pants in public."

During the club's first 10 years, few owned automobiles. To hike places like Maple Canyon near Moroni, White Pine in Little Cottonwood Canyon, and Mutual Dell to Pleasant Grove, they rented trucks and buses. Often the drive was as adventurous as the hike.

"Near the top of the summit (in Parleys Canyon) all the men had to jump out and help push the truck over the other side of the pass," Vanderplas writes. "It was not unusual for a motor vehicle to tip over on its side. No problem. Everyone would scramble out, check for cuts and bruises, and then the men pushed the truck upright again."

Even the Mormon Church was pushing the sport. In a 1921 publication called *The Young Woman's Journal*, an article said girls need to be taught that money is not necessary for a good time. Go hiking instead.

Clothing was to be loose, preferably bloomers, with high-topped shoes or leggings. Heels should be low and broad. Socks should be wool to prevent blisters. Once dressed for hiking, "never permit girls to linger around town where they will attract attention," the article instructs.

"If it is for one night only she can remove her shoes, and sleep in her clothes," the article suggests. "Part of the charm is in the roughing it; and usually one night is enough."

These early women hikers must have been tough. If there was nothing dry to strike a match with, the article recommends "jerking the tip of the match forward against your teeth."

Outdoor recreation had caught fire.

More than 12,000 Utahns were spending a day to a month hiking in canyons from City Creek to American Fork near Highland, according to Robert R.V. Reynolds, a Wasatch National Forest supervisor in 1910.

By 1926, 14,500 boy and girl scouts were camping in Logan Canyon each summer. More than 4,200 families were leasing homes along the Logan River. An estimated 79,000 cars passed through the canyon each year, according to *A History of the Wasatch-Cache National Forest*.

When the Civil Conservation Corps was established in the 1930s to create work for jobless Americans, paths to Mount Olympus, Storm Mountain, Church Fork, Kessler Peak, and Days Fork were improved.

Goodro remembers those days.

"It was more exciting back then," he says. "It was amusing to see the weird outfits; high-laced boots, whipcord riding britches. But they were dedicated to the outdoors."

World War II put the outdoor movement on hold. First came gas rationing. Then men and women went overseas. Many hiking clubs disbanded.

Enthusiam for hiking wasn't renewed until the environmental movement of the '70s and '80s. Since 1987, though, the number of people who hiked or backpacked 52 days or more a year jumped from 381,000 to 799,000 in 1993, according to the Sporting Goods Manufacturers Association.

Winford "Doug" Bludworth of Salt Lake is among them. Forced to take an early retirement from the U.S. Army, 54-year-old Bludworth is hiking the highest point in each state this summer. He has already hiked the tallest points in Utah's counties.

And he has future plans: Hike every point in Utah, outside the Uintas, that is as high or higher than Mt. Timpanogos, at 11,750.

"I've got to where I want to do everything that is high," Bludworth says. "People call me a peak bagger. It's kind of a slam, but I don't mind. Hiking is kind of like alcoholism; you get hooked on it."

GETTING TO THE TOP

After hundreds of miles, 1½ years and the retirement of some hiking boots, two *Salt Lake Tribune* staff writers—Tom Wharton and I—finished "On Top of Utah," a series that chronicled ascents of the highest peak in each of the state's counties.

Twenty-six peaks were bagged. Names were proposed for three summits without monikers during a *Tribune*-sponsored contest. And the same question was posed innumerable times from the public: "What does it take to hike 26 peaks?"

Get in Shape: "It's fun to hike if you are not hurting," said Pat Eisenman, professor in the University of Utah's Department of Exercise and Sport Science. "The better shape you are in, the more you will enjoy it."

Hikers admire the view of Utah Valley from the north peak of Mt. Nebo, Utah County's highest peak. Paula Huff

Start an exercise program at least eight weeks before undertaking a peak. During weeks when a hike is not planned, work out four days. Otherwise, spend three days training and count the trek as the fourth day.

Each exercise session should last an hour: half cardiovascular and the remainder weight training. Aerobic classes, brisk uphill walks, and bicycling uphill while standing—a motion that simulates hiking—are suggestions.

When weight training, divide the time equally between legs and arms. Create a program that concentrates on push-pull lifts that work major muscles. Two days a week, perform 12 to 14 repetitions per exercise with light weight. One day a week, do seven to eight repetitions per exercise with heavier weights.

Correct Equipment: "Durable boots that provide protection and support are the foundation of a hiker's outfit," said Kirk Nichols, faculty member of the University of Utah's Department of Parks, Recreation and Tourism. A shoe made of a single piece of leather wears best, and lug soles provide surer footing. If a boot has lug soles, it will have an adequate midsole, too. This prevents bruises on the foot.

"When I was young, I wore tennis shoes hiking," said 40-year-old Nichols. "At the time, I thought running shoes were wonderful, but I'm paying for that now with stretched ligaments and bone bruises that caused calluses and became painful bone spurs."

A hiking boot should also cradle the foot, preventing stretching when weight is transferred to it. An all-leather boot does. Fabric or running shoes do not.

For clothing, Nichols recommends a three-layer system. First comes the ventilating layer. Made of polyester or polypropylene, it rests against the skin. Because of its nature, water is wicked away from the body. During the summer, cotton often replaces this first layer. Cotton collects perspiration and holds it next to the skin, providing a natural cooling system in the heat. Nichols still carries a polyester top and bottoms in his pack in case the weather turns foul.

Next is the insulating layer in the form of a fleece jacket and pants. In the summer, this is stored in a pack until needed.

Also stored away is the last layer, called the protection layer. Consisting of a jacket and pants, it shields the body from wind and precipitation.

When using the three-layer system, keep your body at a comfortable temperature by adding and removing layers.

Food and Water: "Water is the most important thing," said Janet Anderson, a professor in Utah State University's Department of Nutrition and Food Sciences. "People dehydrate quickly. As soon as you are thirsty, it's too late; you are dehydrated enough that your performance will be affected." To prevent dehydration, drink $\frac{1}{2}$ cup of water every 15 minutes. A water pack with a straw extending toward the mouth makes drinking easier.

For food, Anderson suggests lots of complex carbohydrates, the high-octane fuel source for the human body. A breakfast consisting of cereal, juice, fruit, and toast gives a kick start. Pack more carbohydrates for lunch, such as crackers, bread, low-fat granola bars, dried fruit, and string cheese.

"Stay away from high-fat foods like trail mixes," Anderson said. "They digest slower and make you feel sluggish."

Daypack: Nichols likes a versatile pack. That's why a combination fannypack-knapsack system he devised works. In an extra-large fannypack with a sturdy waist belt he stores a rain jacket, water and lunch. This is used when an hour hike is planned. If headed on a longer trek, he throws on a knapsack that holds more clothing and safety equipment.

"The weight of the knapsack sits on the fannypack, so it feels like I've got on a pack with a real waist-belt system," he said. "I find that this is easier to move in, it provides better ventilation and it gives me the flexibility of carrying how much volume I want to carry."

For safety equipment, Nichols carries disposable butane lighters, a whistle, an 8mm rope that is 40 to 80 feet long, and a pocketknife that has tweezers, a can opener, cutting blade, and screwdriver. A map and compass are part of his pack, too.

Map and compass: Since many of the 26 peaks do not have trails, map reading is necessary. Learn this skill with a 7.5-minute map, available at outdoor stores, the Utah Department of Natural Resource Bookstore, or the USGS Earth Science Information Center, said Bill Case, computer geologist, Utah Geological Survey. At the government stores, a free information sheet called "Topographic Map Symbols" will describe all features on the map.

Start by choosing a 7.5-minute map—also called a topographic map—of an area with which you are familiar. Fold the map in thirds lengthwise, then thirds crosswise so you have a 7-by-6-inch piece of paper.

Locate where you are standing on the map. Place your thumb over the spot, then align the map so features on the land represent features on the map. Start walking, following your course on the map.

"Doing this will give you a perspective of how maps look in relationship to the earth," Case said.

— *Paula Huff*

USING THIS GUIDE

The skills required to reach the highest peak in each of Utah's 29 counties vary from mountain to mountain. In some instances you can drive to within a few feet of the top. Bagging other peaks may require proficiency in mountaineering techniques or map reading.

The beginning of each chapter provides information that can help you prepare for your trip. Each climb is ranked as easy, moderate, or difficult. Criteria used in this rating system are length of the climb, elevation gain, and required route finding skills. Following the rating of the climb is the name of the U.S. Geological Survey 7.5 quadrangle series map that details the area of the climb. These maps are invaluable in helping you find your way, and they can be obtained from the U.S. Geological Survey or from many sporting goods stores. The length of the hike is also noted here. These distances are one-way from the trailhead to the peak.

Each chapter has a locator map with its own legend. These maps provide a general overview of the area around the peak. They show the towns, landmarks, and roads that will help you find your way to the trailhead. These maps are intended to get you started, not to get you to the top; you should have the appropriate U.S. Geological survey map for the hike itself.

Under the "Trailheads" heading you will find a more detailed description of how to find your way. This section will tell you which roads to take, which direction to travel from the nearest town or landmark, and how far it is from point A to point B. This section also provides information on the hike itself. Use this section to find out more about the trail condition, the difficulty of the hike, and what special precautions or skills might be required to reach the top safely.

1 BEAVER AND PIUTE COUNTIES — DELANO PEAK

Summit:	12,169 ft.
Difficulty:	Moderate.
USGS maps:	Delano Peak.
Length:	3.5 miles.

Trailheads: From the Elk Meadows parking lot, this ski tour or hike involves an elevation gain of about 2,500 feet. Hiking the Skyline Trail from Big John Flat involves more of an elevation gain. For one of the tallest peaks in the state, the hike or ski tour is surprisingly easy, but will take up a good part of one day. There can be a danger of avalanches after a heavy snow so taking an avalanche transceiver along as a precaution is a good idea.

Cross-country skiing is available through early June most years. Park at the upper parking lot at the Elk Meadows Ski Resort near the top of Beaver Canyon, east of Beaver. The mountain visible above the resort is Mt. Holly. Work your way around the west side of Mt. Holly and into the saddle that separates that mountain with Delano Peak to the north. Ski up to that ridge and then follow the ridge to the north. Near the top of the rocky peak, you will likely need to take off your skis and walk the last few hundred yards. There is one slightly lower false peak before reaching the highest point, which is marked by a mailbox.

M. Biddle, author of *Fishlake National Forest, Backcountry Guide for Hiking and Horseback Riding*, also suggests finding the Griffin Creek Access to the Skyline Trail, 1.2 miles north of Big John Flat lower in the Canyon. The author suggests walking a half mile in from the trailhead where the pathway narrows and then look up to plan one of several different approaches to the summit. There are no formal trails. Access to the trailheads is also available by driving west on State Highway 153 from Junction off US 89. This road is closed during the winter, however.

The hike: Bob Leonard will never forget the day he worked on a trail near the summit of 12,169-foot Delano Peak in the Tushar Mountains.

"I had packed in a chainsaw with a horse," recalled the archaeologist and trails coordinator for the Fishlake National Forest. "I took the chainsaw and left the horse. When I walked back to get something off the horse, it was gone. There were big cougar tracks where the horse had been." Leonard found the spooked horse unharmed down the canyon.

Brian Head resident Bill Murphy, who has spent much of the past 15 years skiing and hiking peaks throughout southern Utah, has seen Delano under many conditions during different seasons. He calls the hike one of southern Utah's best and most scenic adventures. The peak, the highest in Piute and Beaver counties, straddles the line between the two counties. Murphy tells the story of sharing the windswept peak with a cougar and

BEAVER AND PIUTE COUNTIES — DELANO PEAK

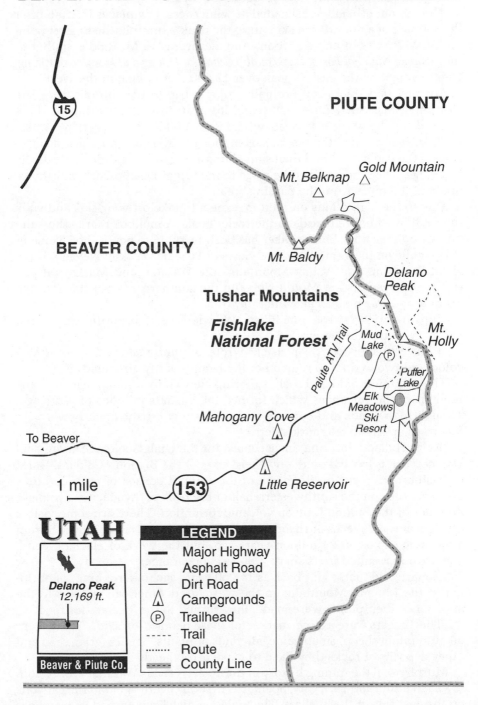

PIUTE COUNTY

BEAVER COUNTY

Gold Mountain

Mt. Belknap

Mt. Baldy

Delano Peak

Tushar Mountains

Fishlake National Forest

Paiute ATV Trail

Mud Lake

Mt. Holly

Puffer Lake

Elk Meadows Ski Resort

Mahogany Cove

To Beaver

1 mile

153

Little Reservoir

UTAH

Delano Peak
12,169 ft.

Beaver & Piute Co.

LEGEND

——	Major Highway
—	Asphalt Road
⊣	Dirt Road
⋀	Campgrounds
Ⓟ	Trailhead
-----	Trail
········	Route
═══	County Line

watching 40 mountain goats forage among the tundra-like grasses above timberline. Elk and mule deer frequent the area.

Though not officially designated as wilderness, few places in Utah offer the solitude of a mid-March ski tour to the peak's summit, the highest point within 110 miles in any direction. And, according to M. Riddle, author of the *Fishlake National Forest Backcountry Guide for Hiking and Horseback Riding*, Delano might be the easiest peak over 12,000 feet to hike in the West.

Murphy said skiers can normally enjoy a trip to the summit from late November until early June each year. Most start from the parking lot of the upper day lodge at the Elk Meadows Ski Resort which is guarded by 11,985-foot Mt. Holly. When the resort is open, nordic skiers can purchase a single ride on the triple chair and then start skiing along the west side of Mt. Holly to a ridge. They then follow the ridge to the top of Delano Peak, a distance of about 3.5 miles from the parking area.

Due to the high winds on the top, expect to take off your skis and walk the final few hundred yards to the rocky peak. A mailbox marks the summit. More than one skier or hiker has been inspired to pen a short verse or story while on the summit, where views of Wheeler Peak in Nevada, Brian Head Peak, the Pine Valley Mountains, the Wasatch and Markagunt plateaus, and even distant Mount Nebo on the southern edge of the Wasatch Front are visible on a clear winter day.

"July 4th, 1994," wrote one hiker. "We witnessed a beautiful sunset that was beyond the human eye."

"I hiked this for two risons [sic]," wrote another visitor. "One to prove I could and two to do it to remember the beauty of my girlfriend."

The summit is bald and rocky, offering views into what appear to be the remains of the volcanoes which formed the Tushars millions of years ago. Though high winds and sun can make the snow crusty, open bowls with few trees appeal to telemark skiers.

Becky Hylland, information specialist for the Utah Geologic Survey, said Delano Peak is located on the northern edge of the Big John Caldera. Dark, reddish-brown rocks on the north of the summit consist of a welded tuft. The gray rock on the southwestern half of the peak is rhyodacite, a younger member of the Bullion Canyon volcanic formation. There are some visible crystals in some pieces of rhyodacite. Delano Peak was created by ash from a volcanic explosion 24 million years ago, but the work of glaciers, wind, and erosion resulted in its sharp, pointed appearance.

Leonard said that, as far back as 14,000 years ago, outcroppings of obsidian in the Mineral Mountains to the west lured American Indians to the area. Once their points were made, they turned to the Tushars for food.

"The Tushars were a supermarket for these people," he said. "There were elk, mountain sheep, small game, all kinds of plants, berries, grass seed and other deposits of rocks they liked to make arrowheads out of."

Murphy said the mining history of the Tushars rivals Wasatch Front boom towns like Alta and Park City. Spaniards first discovered gold in the canyons on the east side of the Tushars. The main Spanish Trail wound its way near

These skiers have abandoned their equipment to make the final approach to Delano Peak, Beaver and Piute counties' highest. Tom Wharton

present-day US 89 between the Tushars and the Markagunt Plateau.

In the 1860s, Brigham Young sent Jacob Hess and a crew to check out the confluence of Pine Creek and the Sevier River in what is now known as Bullion Canyon. They panned the river and found gold. Following Pine Creek up to Bully Boy Flat, they found an arrastra—two stones arranged so they can be dragged across each other to crush rock. This was a tool Spaniards used for mining. Nearby, the settlers found two rotten leather sacks filled with gold ore.

Rell Frederick, a historian and present-day Marysvale miner, said that when the Mormons found the arrastra, they also found veins containing high-grade gold. Once the precious metal was found, the population exploded. Some 2,000 residents lived in Bullion at an elevation of 9,000 feet and the boom town soon became the Piute County seat. Today, there are only 1,200 residents in the entire county.

"The whole region was honeycombed with rich ore," wrote Dale Morgan, Utah historian. "Miners and promoters poured into the area. The eastern part of Beaver County was the solid, aloof Mormon farmers and stock-raisers. In the western part were the brawling, fortune-hunting miners." Famed outlaw Butch Cassidy once worked in the Bullion area.

Though Frederick has lost a brother and a lung to the work, mining still holds an attraction.

"Word-of-mouth records of gold nuggets being found in the Tushars that are as large as a big man's fist," he said. "Then, of course, playing in the mine and being on the hill is better than working for a living."

Frederick and other Marysvale miners gather every Tuesday afternoon to swap stories, talk mining, and play cards. One yearly event for the group is the hunt for a can of gold lost from the Tushars' Wedge Mine.

In the 1930s, several men camped at the 11,000-foot-high mine, intending to prospect through the winter. All the miners agreed to put the gold they found in a can, planning to split it after winter. One man named Tahay became sick. The other miners put him on a sleigh and had a horse or dog pull him down the hill for medical help. When the snow ran out, Tahay tied the sleigh to three trees, and carved a star in one of the trees.

The evening Tahay left camp the other miners went to put their gold in the can and it was gone. Tayhay died a few days later, never revealing the whereabouts of the gold.

"In 1962, a snowslide brought his sleigh out of the mountains, and that started the looking all over again," said Frederick.

A few mines remain open on a small scale. Many old-time miners, such as Marysvale dairy farmer Joel Johnson, still spend their free time prospecting with a wheelbarrow and shovel.

"I'm actually a dairy farmer," said the 66-year-old Johnson. "The mine I've got is kind of a hobby. Actually, it's quite hard work for a man my age."

These days, visitors looking for a taste of the old mining atmosphere can drive six miles west of Marysvale up Bullion Canyon to a miner's park. There, visitors can enjoy looking at old mining equipment, a rebuilt portal and shaft, a hiking trail, and car tour.

Cattle and sheep graze the lower meadows below Delano Peak. In the summer, the top of Beaver Canyon is popular with campers, hikers, and ATV users who enjoy the nearby Paiute ATV trail.

Delano Peak was named for Columbus Delano, who was the secretary of the interior under President U.S. Grant. The Tushar Mountains were so named because of the imagined resemblance of the peaks to the tusks of the boar, although legend also suggests there was an ancient tribe of Indians who lived there named the Tushari.

— Paula Huff and Tom Wharton

---

2   *BOX ELDER COUNTY — BULL MOUNTAIN*

Summit: 9,920 ft.
Difficulty: Moderate.
USGS maps: Rosevere Point, Standrod.
Length: 4.5 miles.

Trailhead: The Raft River Mountains are surrounded by private land. One of the few legal accesses is Clear Creek. Get to Clear Creek by heading west from Snowville on State Route 30. After 18 miles, turn onto State Route 42 at a junction. About 8.5 miles down this road you will see a small, green "Strevell Road 3600 South" sign. Turn onto this gravel road and drive three miles to the Clear Creek Campground turn off. Drive six miles on the dirt road to the campground. The trailhead, marked Bull Flat, is at the end of the campground. It can be used by hikers, horses, mountain bikes, and all-terrain vehicles. About a mile into the hike there is a Bull Flat turn off. Bypass this and continue to the Lake Fork junction, where you take a right. This takes you to Bull Lake. There is a faint trail to the right of the Bull Lake cirque that takes you on top. Once there, look for a building that sits on Bull Mountain.

The hike: Wayne Pugsley was cowpunching on the nearly 10,000-foot rolling flat tops of the Raft River Mountains once when he was offered a ride home—on a hang glider.

"The hang glider said he could drop me off at home, but I was never brave enough to do it," said Pugsley, a 37-year-old who has spent his life firmly planted on his Park Valley ranch. "He said he glided to Black Pine one day, which is 20 miles away. Another day he planned to make it to Pocatello—100 miles."

Hang gliding is new to this range, which hosts Box Elder County's highest peak, Bull Mountain, at 9,920 feet. Surrounding canyons are wide and lush with perennial streams in the bottom. At the base, pinyons mix with mountain mahogany, then sweep up to conifers.

To get to Bull Mountain, Box Elder County's highest peak, one must walk around the cirque that forms Bull Lake. Paula Huff

Cattle raising, sheep grazing, and mining are more conventional uses. Hunters and all-terrain vehicle enthusiasts flock to the rolling hills and maze of roads.

Long ago, American Indians roamed the land. Pine nuts drew Goshutes and their predecessors the Fremont to the Raft Rivers, situated in the northwest corner of the state. The Great Basin's northern- and eastern-most fingers of pine nut-bearing single leaf pinyons stretch to these mountains then stop. Munching these sweet, edible seeds earned the Indians the name "tubaduka"—pine nut eaters. Gathering excursions also collected chokecherries, game, and insects as food.

Deer and other big game are what most people assume that American Indians hunted, but bushy-tail squirrels and marmots were considered delicacies. The crop-devouring locusts that were a scourge to early white settlers were manna from heaven for Goshutes.

"They [Goshutes] would have seen the crickets as calories raining down," said Utah State Paleoecologist David Madsen. "These were flexible and adaptable people. Where the farming was good they grew corn, beans, squash, and collected wild animals and plants. Where it was too hot to farm, they were hunters and gathers."

Pine nut trips to the Raft Rivers didn't stop with American Indians. Many long-time Park Valley ranchers remember family outings in search of the seeds. And there was another annual summer trip that still has grandparents reminiscing.

"For the Fourth of July we used to go into the mountains with a saddle

BOX ELDER COUNTY — BULL MOUNTAIN

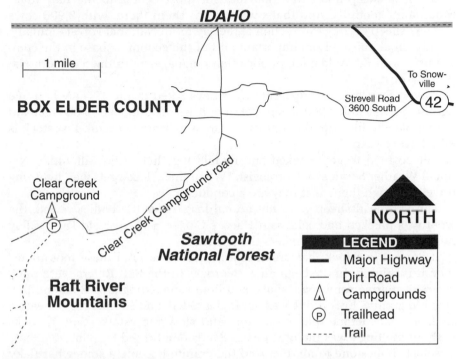

IDAHO

1 mile

BOX ELDER COUNTY

To Snow-ville

Strevell Road
3600 South

42

Clear Creek
Campground

Clear Creek Campground road

Sawtooth
National Forest

Raft River
Mountains

NORTH

LEGEND
▬	Major Highway
—	Dirt Road
⚠	Campgrounds
Ⓟ	Trailhead
-----	Trail

Bull Mountain — close up

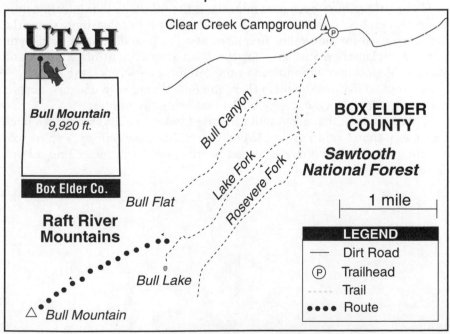

UTAH

Bull Mountain
9,920 ft.

Box Elder Co.

Raft River
Mountains

Clear Creek Campground Ⓟ

Bull Canyon

Lake Fork

Rosevere Fork

BOX ELDER
COUNTY

Sawtooth
National Forest

1 mile

Bull Flat

Bull Lake

△ Bull Mountain

LEGEND
—	Dirt Road
Ⓟ	Trailhead
-----	Trail
●●●●	Route

horse and pack bags, said Max Kunzler, a 77-year-old rancher. "We would fill the pack bags with snow and carry it back to town to make ice cream."

But it is sheep and cattle that brought most people to the Raft River Mountains' foothills. And that's what keeps them there, with 2,906 cows and 957 sheep grazing this section of the Sawtooth National Forest annually.

"Livestock raising is an important part of the economic base in the community," said Ed Waldapfel, public-affairs manager with the Sawtooth National Forest.

Wayne Pugsley's grandparents were devastated in the 1940s when one lightning strike killed 900 sheep. Bereft of trees high up, over 9,000 feet and with a plateau-like top, the Raft Rivers are a lightning beacon. Livestock is killed every year.

"Sheep tend to get spooked and huddle together," said Bill Alder, National Weather Service meteorologist. "When their fleece gets wet, lightning travels through them as if they are a conductor."

The 900 dead sheep were not a total loss. After the bodies rotted, the wool was plucked and sold, said Harvey Carter, a 78-year-old Park Valley rancher who clearly remembers the incident.

If it's not livestock that provides a livelihood around these mountains, then it is mining. In the beginning, the rocks of the Raft Rivers were thick layers of marine sandstone, shale, and limestone sitting atop 2,500-million year old granite. Everything was uplifted, eroded, and submerged beneath a shallow sea. Metamorphose—heating and slow recrystallization of rocks without melting—was the next phase. Sandstone turned to quartzite. Shale to schist. Limestone to marble. And the granite became a somewhat flaky rock called gneiss.

Though there have been gold mines, it is the quartzite that interests miners in this east-west mountain range. Called Raft River flagstone, these flat rocks are used for sidewalks, fireplaces and the face of houses, said Lynn Kunzler, reclamation specialist for the Utah Department of Oil, Gas and Mining. Magnesium, graphite and tungsten mines also pock the range.

Miners and livestock owners share the Raft Rivers with cougars, coyote, bobcat and deer. It's the trophy bucks that bring the hunters.

"There is a rock that my grandfather used to look behind and find a buck deer every time," said Pugsley. "My father did the same thing, and he told me about it. But now there is a road nearby, and I can never find a buck there anymore."

— Paula Huff

3 CACHE COUNTY — NAOMI PEAK

Summit:	9,979 ft.
Difficulty:	Easy.
USGS map:	Naomi Peak.
Length:	2.75 miles.

Trailhead: From the Canyon Entrance Park at the mouth of Logan Canyon, drive 19.1 miles up the canyon to the Tony Grove Lake turnoff. Take this left turn and drive another 7 miles on a paved road to the parking lot. In winter this road is usually plowed, though not all the way to the parking lot. Using a map, look northeast to Mt. Magog, the rocky peak on the horizon. Begin by skiing toward this peak. The summer hiking trail heads this direction, too. If you know it, that trail is a safe route for the first mile. To avoid cliffs and avalanches, begin walking ridge lines leading to Mt. Magog. Less than half a mile from Magog, notice a northwest ridge heading toward Naomi Peak to the left. Follow this ridge, with one last steep climb, until you reach the flat top heading directly to Naomi. This ridge will have large cornices.

Though a beautiful wildflower-strewn trail in the summer, this tour is extremely difficult in the winter because of many cliffs and avalanche-slide paths. Hundreds of snowmobilers also make use of this area in the winter months.

The hike: "Tony" is 1920s slang for high-class. And in 1880, it was the socially elite who frolicked in Tony Grove 19 miles up Logan Canyon, giving the meadow and lake its name. Now this grove is a trailhead to Cache County's highest peak—Naomi Peak.

At 9,979 feet, Naomi Peak is an amphitheater for a geologic opera. Basin and range guard the west. The Uinta Mountains loom in the southeast. Wyoming's high plateau country is northeast. And on a clear day, the rugged Tetons can be seen.

Named by a homesick government surveyor in the 1870s who wanted to commemorate his wife, the view from the top offers a peek into history.

Logan Canyon is an ancient aquarium that has turned to stone. One mile deep in places, the gorge is limestone—a storehouse for marine creatures 500 to 200 million years old. Frozen in rock are the skeletons of horned corals, reef corals, trilobites, brachiopods, clams, crinoids, and fish scales. The deeper gray the limestone, the more fossils.

Glaciers that once covered Naomi Peak in the Bear River Range left marks, too. While the ice was melting 14,000 years ago, five canyons were eroded into the peak's sides. In the wake is a jumble of cliffs, basins, canyons, small hills and lakes. Tony Grove Lake is one remnant.

Though the glaciers are long gone, Logan Canyon and the Cache Valley it drains into remain marshy and wet. This water was a mecca for plants, animals, birds, fish and, eventually, humans, 11,000 years ago.

British fur trappers searching for beaver entered Cache Valley in 1812. Famous trappers such as Jim Bridger followed. All found the elusive dam-building creatures, along with many American Indians hunting buffalo and other food sources such as fish, roots, fruits, and berries. Shoshone were the predominant band, according to Gordon Cole's *History of Cache Valley to 1859*.

Few of these early people ever traveled through Logan Canyon, though, even though it is the most direct modern-day route to Naomi Peak. Trapper Warren Angus Ferris gives a clue why in his 1832 diary. It took two days to go through a "narrow defile, nearly impassable to equestrians," Ferris said of the canyon named for a trapper killed during a skirmish with American Indians.

"We were often compelled while struggling over the defile, to cross the stream and ford our way through almost impenetrable thickets, and at times, to follow a narrow trail along the borders of precipices, where a single mis-step would inevitably have sent horse and rider to the shades of death."

There were easier routes into Cache Valley, such as Strawberry Canyon to the north and Blacksmith Fork Canyon to the south. Mormons seeking new grazing land away from drought-wracked central Utah finally entered Cache Valley in 1855 from the south.

Still, Logan Canyon was little used until 1862, when spiritual leader Brigham Young instructed followers to build a temple and tabernacle in Logan for The Church of Jesus Christ of Latter-Day Saints, according to historian A.J. Simmonds. Logan Canyon's ruggedness had preserved its tim-ber, now needed for the temple. There were also stone quarries and lime-stone for making masonry. Road work started during the spring of 1862. By summer, heavy runoff had washed out all the bridges. Little follow-up work occurred until 1865. Fifteen years later, the 41-mile road finally ended at Bear Lake.

Trees soon became railroad ties, telegraph poles, scaffolding poles and lumber. Canyon names still reflect this 20-year era—"China Row" for an area where Asian railroad builders camped, and "Temple Fork" where logs were taken for the edifice.

All this activity introduced whole families to the canyon. Mormon men sent to work at sawmills had their wives and children visit. There were Sunday religious services, holiday celebrations, and dancing every day of the week.

Charles O. Card, supervisor of the temple construction, remembers a visit when millhands were square dancing. A bow tied on the arm indicated which men played the role of "lady," according to Melvin A. Larkin in *The History of the LDS Temple in Logan, Utah*. Benjamin Wilmore remembers the time in his personal notes called *Some Early Experiences in Logging in Logan Canyon*.

"Some times a log with a good smooth snow surface to slide on would go with terrific speed and very erratic as to the course depending on the hills, indentations of the mountain side," wrote Wilmore. "The timber would go

CACHE COUNTY — NAOMI PEAK

IDAHO

Bear Lake

High Creek
South Fork

△ *Mount Gog*

△ *Mount Magog*

Naomi Peak △

Cherry Creek

Ⓟ *Tony Grove*
Lake

Bear River Range

Tony Grove
Lake turnoff

🛡️ **89**

Wasatch-Cache
National Forest

CACHE COUNTY

Logan Canyon

▲ *Logan*

▲
NORTH

LEGEND
— Asphalt Road
Ⓟ Car Park
- - - Trail
▬▬▬ Stateline
••••• Winter Route

1 mile
⊢—⊣

UTAH

Naomi Peak
9,979 ft.

Cache Co.

Naomi Peak, Cache County's highest peak, is often covered with snow on Memorial Day. Paula Huff

downward with bullet speed and sometimes would strike a bump and fly through the air a long distance, with a successful landing on the mountain side or in the river below. Sometimes the timber was shattered into kindling wood."

Though logging may have denuded the canyon, it also opened up the area for recreation. Logan Sheriff Nick Crookston remembers heading for the mountains on a road only slightly better than a trail. A wagon was loaded with supplies, while the women and children rode in a white-topped buggy.

The Moses Thatcher family, known for its banking services in Logan, camped at Tony Grove for six weeks each summer. Helen Mar Kimball Whitney, a polygamous wife of a Salt Lake Mormon, wrote letters about one trip with the Thatcher family.

"Whitney and her companions explored Logan Cave, wandered playfully across giant fallen logs in the river, climbed on the sage and juniper hillsides surrounding Ricks Springs, and finally made camp near Tony Grove," writes Paige Lewis in her master's thesis *I Just Grew Up Loving the Canyon: Logan Canyon and the Influence of Place on Personal History.* "The next morning the women cooked hot biscuits, fried fish, and coffee for breakfast while the men prepared for another day of fishing." One picture from a Thatcher trip shows two women leaning against boulders with butterfly nets flung over their shoulders.

When the timber was gone, cattle and sheep were led up the canyon. Tony Grove was a favorite campsite for cowboys. And sheepherders used the area so often that 19 years after a sheep-dipping operation ended, the meadow was a dust bowl that still smelled of the creosote used for ridding livestock of ticks and mites, according to Soren Peterson in a speech titled "Some Memories of Early Days in Logan, Utah 1866–1902."

People exploring the canyon during the early part of the 20th century began making discoveries. One was the Jardine Juniper, a tree found by Maurice Linford in 1923. Named after then agriculture secretary William M. Jardine, it is nearly 3,000 years old.

Another find was "Old Ephraim," the last known grizzly in the Cache National Forest. After raiding Frank Clark's sheep herd for years, the bear was killed on Aug. 22, 1923. His skull is at the Smithsonian Institute.

A few years earlier, the last five elk in the Bear River Range were killed in Card Canyon. Logan citizens purchased two boxcar loads from Jackson Hole, Wyoming to re-establish the herd. The elk were "penned on a corner of Tabernacle Square...," writes Charles S. Peterson in *A History of the Wasatch-Cache National Forest, 1903–1980*.

"When ticks began to plague the herd, local farmers, worried that the parasites threatened their dairy herd and livestock, complained bitterly."

The elk were driven to the mouth of Logan Canyon and turned loose. That herd is healthy now, along with other animal populations such as deer, blue grouse, rough grouse, snowshoe rabbit, Hungarian partridge, chuckars, sage hen, and cottontail. Moose mill about Tony Grove Lake.

Logan Canyon is now the domain of recreationists: campers, bikers, hikers, anglers, hunters, and rock climbers. And for the adventurous, there is even cave exploring. Water dissolves limestone, leaving behind caves and sinkholes. There are more than 20 at Tony Grove. Clair Wyatt of Logan has explored some.

"I went in one once," Wyatt recalls. "It was like going down into a milk bottle. It was narrow at first, then I was dangling in free space. It was the scariest thing in my life."

— *Paula Huff*

4 CARBON COUNTY — MONUMENT PEAK

Summit:	10,452 ft.
Difficulty:	Easy (a good mountain bike ride).
USGS map:	Scofield, Candland Mountain.
Length:	Drive to within a few feet of the top.

Trailhead: On US Route 6 between Spanish Fork and Price, take the Scofield/ Scofield State Park/Clear Creek turnoff. This puts you on US Route 96 going south. Drive 23 miles to the intersection with Clear Creek, but continue toward Fairview. This road is now US Route 264 going west. From the intersection drive about 5 miles to the Emery County boundary sign and the summit of Eccles Canyon. This puts you on Trough Springs Ridge. Park and begin skiing on the snow-covered dirt road to the left. Follow this road until it crosses the ridge leading to Monument Peak, then hike to the summit, which has a hut with a radio tower on top and a large rock cairn. This area is used heavily by snowmobilers.

Skiing this peak is strenuous. From the trailhead, it is downhill until the peak's base, then a quarter-mile trek up. This would be better as a scenic drive or a mountain bike ride. Another hiking option is to approach from Long Canyon out of Clear Creek.

The hike: Step out of a car at Clear Creek. Sniff the air. Examine the black specks on the snow. That, alone, should reveal much about this area's history. This is coal country.

Clear Creek is three miles from the highest peak in Carbon County, Monument Peak (10,452 feet). Mine roads, gas lines and railroad tracks crisscross the land. Steel machinery and old buildings appear at every turn.

But coal isn't the only thing extracted from the earth around here. A few miles away in Huntington Canyon, a construction worker discovered a Columbian mammothin 1990. The 10,600-year-old skeleton was found in an ancient bog, among spearheads made by paleo-Indians. Fremont Indian camp sites nearby show that while hunting elk, deer and mountain sheep, coal was used.

When U.S. Gen. William H. Ashley entered the area now known as Carbon County in 1825, he saw American Indians. The land was barren and almost entirely devoid of game.

"We saw a few mountain sheep and some elk," he recorded in his diary. "I met some Eutau tribe Indians, who appeared very glad to see us and treated us in a friendly manner. These Indians were well-dressed in skins, had some guns but armed generally with bows and arrows and such other instruments of war as are found among Indians of the Missouri.... They have no fixed place of residence but roam from place to place."

Utah County immigrants began taking livestock into the Scofield and

CARBON COUNTY — MONUMENT PEAK

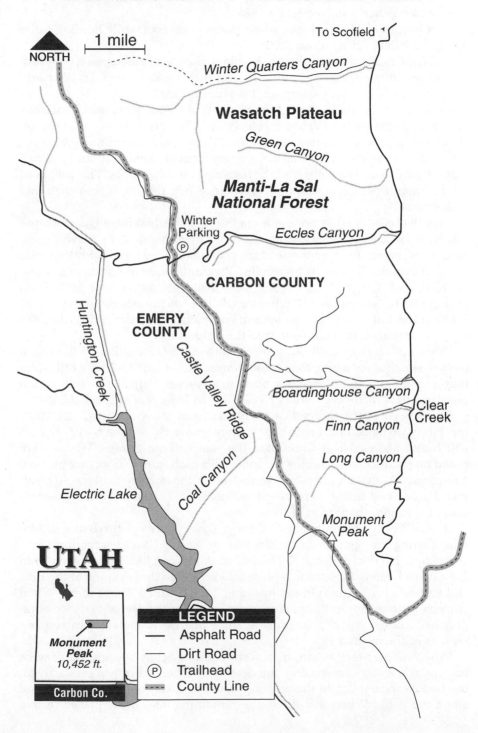

1 mile

NORTH

To Scofield

Winter Quarters Canyon

Wasatch Plateau

Green Canyon

Manti-La Sal National Forest

Winter Parking

Ⓟ

Eccles Canyon

CARBON COUNTY

EMERY COUNTY

Huntington Creek

Castle Valley Ridge

Boardinghouse Canyon

Clear Creek

Finn Canyon

Long Canyon

Coal Canyon

Electric Lake

Monument Peak

UTAH

Monument Peak
10,452 ft.

Carbon Co.

LEGEND
— Asphalt Road
— Dirt Road
Ⓟ Trailhead
County Line

Clear Creek country in the areas below Monument Peak to graze on the luxuriant native grasses by 1877. Two sawmills were cutting timber a year later, and another was erected by 1881.

As a boy, Isaac Morely Jones wrote that he saw coal while herding cattle along the White River in the 1870s.

"...While riding through the thick cedars, the men came upon a coal vein uncovered by the river. We built a fire on it to cook our supper. We could not put the fire out, and I suppose it is still burning."

Geologic events that created Monument Peak country happened millions of years ago during the Carboniferous Period. The area was once a swamp. When plants died, they rotted in the water. Then the Earth's climate changed. Mountains were pushed upward. Canyons formed. Sand and mud washed down by snow and rain covered the decaying swamp plants. The weight of the sediments pressed the spongy mass together, turning it into rock that became coal.

And that coal is what drew miners by 1878, with Winter Quarters one mile west of Scofield being Carbon County's first boom. When railway companies discovered the magnitude of the coal fields, they thoroughly explored every canyon leading to the area called Pleasant Valley in search of a route. Spanish Fork Canyon was chosen, and a narrow gauge was built from Springville to Scofield in 1879. Before the line was finished, winter set in. The last few miles were laid on ice and snow since deep drifts had filled the canyon, making it impossible to find the ground.

"This was all right until the severe weather was succeeded by the warm days of spring... for a long time trains coming into town could not tell when they would be able to leave, for upon nearly every trip the engine would require a new road bed," writes J.W. Dilley in *History of the Scofield Mine*.

In the wake of the railroad came miners from many countries. By 1900, the Finns, Italians, and English at Winter Quarters swelled to 1,500 with 250 frame homes. Clear Creek had the same ethnic groups. Wages were based on production—43 cents per ton—with each miner supplying his own equipment. Wallace's ancestors were among those early settlers. A great-grandfather and uncle were killed in the May 1, 1900, Winter Quarters Mine explosion, the largest of those days.

It was Dewey Day in honor of George Dewey, hero of the Battle of Manila. During the Spanish-American War he had led the destruction of an entire Spanish fleet without the loss of an American life. Miners went into the cavern looking forward to a program and dance that evening at the new Old Fellow's Hall. An explosion just after 10 A.M. killed 200 of them. When citizens in town heard the ruckus, many thought the Dewey Day celebration had started early. Then miners from nearby tunnels began sending reports of the mishap.

When rescue work began, men were piled in heaps because there were not enough volunteers to carry the dead out. When more workers arrived, the bodies were taken to the meeting house and laid out on the stand and along the walls. When that filled, the remaining dead were placed in two

A road near Monument Peak, Carbon County's highest, makes it an easy walk in the summer. Make it more challenging by skiing or mountain bike riding to the summit. Paula Huff

rooms of the school.

The chief storekeeper for the Pleasant Valley Coal Company hurried to Salt Lake City to buy coffins and clothing for the dead. Each was dressed in underclothes, a white shirt and collar, necktie and elegant black suit. There were not enough coffins in the state's capital, so more were ordered from Denver, Colo. J.A. Lambert of Ogden wrote that 10 of his relatives were killed; one buried under the debris was never found.

"My God it is awful. No tongue or pen can describe the horror of the situation down there.... Whole families are wiped out and the women do nothing but shriek and wring their hands day and night. There are pitiful sights and cases there that would stir the hearts of the most callous. Take an instance—that of Mrs. Williams, who came from Tennessee with her husband and a family of seven children a few days before the explosion. Her husband went to work in the mine and the next day met his death there."

Under the direction of teacher Mrs. E.L. Carpenter, students from Salt Lake City sent three railroad cars of flowers to Scofield. As each wagon carrying a coffin moved past these cars, the casket was buried under lilacs, pansies, violets, geraniums, roses, carnations, Easter lilies, asparagus ferns, tulips, flowering almonds and fruit blossoms.

Since many of the mine's workers were killed and others refused to return to work, new workers were hired. But, they wanted better working conditions and started strikes and called for unions. In an oral history from

1976, Howard Stevens recalls when 200 Winter Quarters miners protested.

"They went on strike and the company brought in a lot of Chinamen to work. Do you know what those old miners did? They loaded them [the Chinese] in a boxcar and turned it loose down the track," Stevens said. "I never did hear what happened to that, but I guess it scared those old Chinamen out and they never did come back."

To forget work-day troubles, these miners turned to the mountains. Many fished. Wallace remembers long horseback rides with her brother near Monument Peak. In the shadow of this mountain, her parents picked raspberries for jam. There was a ski hill, including a rope tow, just above Clear Creek. But it was the ball diamond that drew the crowds.

"There was a grandstand with chicken wire all over it so the balls wouldn't hit people," Wallace said. "There was a team in Scofield, Clear Creek, Soldier Summit and Helper. There was always free pop—mostly root beer—and ice cream cones."

Another favorite pastime was "sham battles." Men, women and children would dress as Indians or pioneers.

"The pioneers would circle their wagons, and the Indians would come out of Ball Diamond Canyon, attack the wagons and burn them," Wallace said, laughing.

When the mines began closing during the 1920s, people left. Homes were torn down, buried or washed away by floods. The ski hill closed. A sewer treatment plant covered the ball diamond. Winter Quarters is nonexistent.

White Oak and Skyline Mine still extract coal from Eccles Canyon near Monument Peak. Most workers live in Price, where their children can attend school. In Utah, there are only 12 active coal mines, with most used for power plants or making steel in the Far East.

Clear Creek and Scofield are the domain of anglers during the summer and snowmobiles during the winter. But the smell of coal is still heavy in the air. Many still use it to heat their homes.

"We get a ton or two of coal and it lasts us a year," Wallace said. "It's $28 a ton and that's high. I remember when a load of coal was $3."

— *Paula Huff*

5 DAGGETT AND UINTAH COUNTIES — ECCENTRIC PEAK

> **Summit:** 12,276 ft.
> **Difficulty:** Moderate.
> **USGS maps:** Chepeta Lake, Whiterocks Lake.
> **Length:** 2 miles.

Trailhead: From Main Street in Roosevelt, turn north on 200 North. Drive about 10 miles to a four-way stop. Continue straight for seven miles until reaching a road marked Elkhorn-Whiterocks. Turn right. Drive 5.2 miles to a T-intersection. Turn left toward Elkhorn. Drive 3.1 miles to a Y-intersection. Stay left, going toward Elkhorn. After 1.1 miles, make a left turn at a sign marked Elkhorn Loop Road, Pole Creek Lake, Chepeta Lake and Uinta Canyon. After 13 miles, turn right at a Chepeta Lake sign. Drive 3.6 miles and take another right to Chepeta Lake. Drive another 6.8 miles to a stream crossing the road about .25 mile from Chepeta Lake. Most years, four-wheel drive is needed to cross this stream. Park and walk to Chepeta Lake.

There is no trail to Eccentric Peak. A map and compass are absolutely necessary in this rolling landscape. The east side of Chepeta Lake is a cliff/talus slope. Backtrack a short distance southeast until seeing a faint trail that climbs above this cliff/talus slope. At the top of the cliff/talus slope, the trail disappears. Eccentric Peak is not obvious. Begin route finding across high alpine meadows in a northeast direction toward a low point on the ridge that overlooks Daggett Lake. From here, hike east in this gently climbing landscape for about 1 mile until reaching a rock shelter that marks Eccentric Peak.

The hike: It's the landscape where Butch Cassidy once cooked and served Thanksgiving dinner to ranch families. Where men hunting dinosaur bones drew guns over territorial disputes. And where soldiers once marched across the Uinta Mountains mid-winter to prevent an army and its livestock from starving.

Eccentric also has the distinction of being the highest peak in Uintah and Daggett counties at 12,276 feet. To the north of this wide talus summit, Flaming Gorge Dam's plug on the Green River has backed water into Wyoming. Kings Peak, Utah's highest, rises to the west. And a glance over any brink reveals lakes strung together by streams in wide valleys. As a youngster, this was Leta Wahlquist's back yard.

"When I was around 6 years old, my older sisters and cousins would pack our horses and go on the mountain," said Wahlquist, who returned to her hometown of Manila a few years ago to work as Daggett County's jailer. "We'd pitch our tent and stay for a week. We'd scramble eggs with shredded wheat to make something like a stiff pancake. We took cans of fruit, and kept milk in cool streams."

For entertainment the all-female excursion would float inner tubes in a meandering stream now flooded by Long Park Reservoir. Fish were so plentiful they could be scooped into a washtub for dinner.

That was then.

In 1994, Flaming Gorge Dam ranked fourth as the most visited recreation area in Utah, with 1.9 million sightseers yearly. Temple Square, Lake Powell and Zion National Park were the top three respectively. But a brief walk above popular water holes—like Flaming Gorge or Spirit and Chepeta lakes at Eccentric Peak's base—and the country is empty, the scenery big.

The Uinta Mountain's rolling vistas started as Precambrian sandstone and shale, so old that when deposited by an ocean 600 million years ago living organisms did not have skeletons, said Andy Godfrey, a geomorphologist for the USDA Forest Service in Ogden. About 70 million years ago, the landscape pushed upward, tilting slightly toward the south. Glaciers formed a half million years ago, then completely melted about 10,000 years ago, leaving broad U-shaped valleys scooped out by creeping ice.

"The cold nights, short summers and permanent snowbanks give the impression that the climate in the High Uintas is not far from glacial conditions," said Godfrey. "In fact, scientists consider some features on the landscape indicative of periglacial, or near glacial conditions. Intense frost action and repeated freezing and thawing of the ground have produced a series of features that are unique to arctic and alpine areas."

A periglacial feature known as "patterned ground" covers Eccentric Peak. When soil freezes several feet deep, water inside turns to ice and expands. This expansion heaves large rocks up through the earth to the surface. These stones topple off the uplifted ground and accumulate in depressions. High alpine grasses grow on the raised patches of dirt, making the landscape look like a muffin tin from above. Where the ground is flat, individual patterns created by these frost-heaved rocks are called stone polygons. Several linked together form a stone net. Where the land slopes, the polygons stretch into stone stripes.

American Indians moved these rocks to make depressions where they hid while stalking game, said Krista Malmstrom, archaeological technician for the Ashley National Forest. Malmstrom and colleagues have spent three summers walking Ashley National Forest looking for artifacts left by these people.

"We've found some large knives: 5-inches long, oval shaped and made of tiger chert, which is black and tan banded," Malmstrom said. "When you see a nice big knife made of that you just say, 'Wow, that is art.' "

Trappers found the Eccentric Peak area attractive for another reason: beaver. One of their first rendezvous in the early 1800s was on the summit's east flank near Browns Park. The area became a favorite over-wintering site and later the town of Linwood, Utah. The state's oldest town is now under Flaming Gorge's water.

By 1857, Col. Albert Sidney Johnston and his army arrived at Wyoming's

DAGGETT AND UINTAH COUNTIES —
ECCENTRIC PEAK

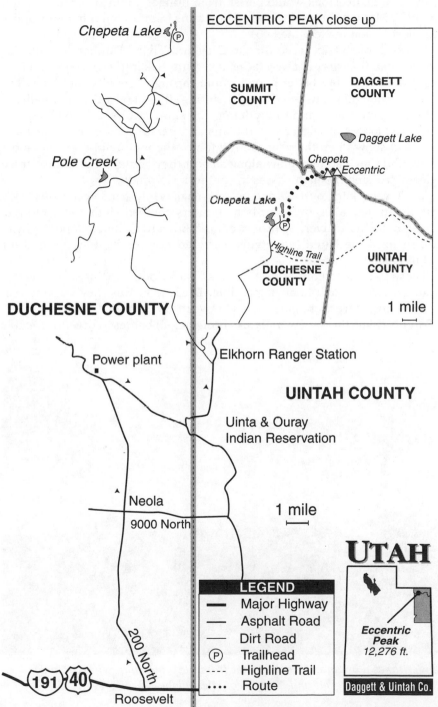

Chepeta Lake

ECCENTRIC PEAK close up

SUMMIT
COUNTY

DAGGETT
COUNTY

Daggett Lake

Pole Creek

Chepeta
Eccentric

Chepeta Lake

Highline Trail

UINTAH
COUNTY

DUCHESNE
COUNTY

DUCHESNE COUNTY

1 mile

Elkhorn Ranger Station

Power plant

UINTAH COUNTY

Uinta & Ouray
Indian Reservation

Neola
9000 North

1 mile

200 North

LEGEND

— Major Highway
— Asphalt Road
— Dirt Road
Ⓟ Trailhead
---- Highline Trail
.... Route

191 40

Roosevelt

UTAH

Eccentric
Peak
12,276 ft.

Daggett & Uintah Co.

Fort Bridger with orders to subdue Mormons rebelling against the federal government. When church members heard about the plans, they set traps, including burning the nearby prairie to destroy livestock fodder. When it looked as if all livestock would perish from hunger, Johnston ordered Capt. Randolph Marcy to cross the Uinta Mountains in mid-winter to get supplies from Fort Union in New Mexico.

"It was a rough trip," according to Dick and Vivian Dunham's book *Our Strip of Land: A History of Daggett County*. "[Jim] Baker [the guide] was all for taking the easier and better-known route through Brown's [sic] Hole, but Marcy insisted they must save time by cutting straight over the mountains.... As they neared the summit they found the snow two feet deep. They ran onto three lodges of Digger Ute Indians and persuaded one of them to go along and show them the way. On the top of the mountain their guide deserted, and they had to wallow along as best they could, ...but almost froze to death crossing the high passes in southern Colorado."

Just 20 years later, outlaws and paleontologists inhabited Eccentric Peak's foothills. In the 1870s, dinosaur-bone hunters combed Utah. Once Othniel C. Marsh, a Yale University professor, and Edward Drinker Cope, a physician, realized the Uinta Mountains harbored few fossils, they headed for Uintah Basin's cache.

"These two started out as best friends," said Godfrey. "But each was trying to gather as much fame as possible. Because of this they became real enemies, and there were gun battles between their crews."

Bandits riding the outlaw trails also brought gun battles to Eccentric Peak's

A hiker takes a break in a rock shelter from the winds that whip around Eccentric Peak, Daggett and Uintah counties' highest. Paula Huff

lowlands. Browns Park was a favorite hangout for fugitives, according to Michael Johnson, who is writing Daggett County's history for the state centennial. Butch Cassidy, Matt Warner and Harry Longabaugh (also known as the Sundance Kid) among others made this their home when running from the law.

"Browns Park people thought the world of Butch Cassidy," said Johnson. The affection was reciprocated, as shown by an 1895 Thanksgiving dinner he and other outlaws prepared for 35 Browns Park ranch families. They "did not spare expenses in putting over a grand spread of the best delicacies Rock Springs [Wyoming] could supply," according to Ann Bassett in *The Bassett Women*.

Now, the outlaws are gone, the paleontologists are more civilized, and tourists swarm their stomping grounds. But one thing has remained the same over these generations: the Uinta Mountain's consistent weather.

Morning skies in the Uinta Mountains are often clear. When the sun begins heating the ground, it makes the atmosphere "boil like a pot of water," said David Hogan, meteorologist for the National Weather Service in Salt Lake City. Rising hot air carries moisture upward and thunderstorms brew. Summer winds from the southwest push air into the mountains, which lifts and acts as another kick start for rain clouds. Late afternoon skies in the Uintas become heavy with moisture and a series of squalls ensue. By evening, the atmosphere cools and clouds dissipate. The next morning, another bluebird day dawns.

— *Paula Huff*

6 DAVIS AND MORGAN COUNTIES — THURSTON PEAK

Summit: 9,707 ft.
Difficulty: Easy.
USGS map: Peterson.
Length: 3.5 miles.

Trailhead: On Farmington's Main Street, head east. Turn north on 100 East. This leads directly to Farmington Canyon, a well-maintained, but cliff-perched road. After seven miles, the road splits. Take the north fork to the radar station domes, about six miles. On the north side of the domes, find the trailhead that follows the ridgeline north to Thurston Peak.

The hike: While cutting trees in the mountains east of Centerville, Thomas Jefferson Thurston looked from the ridgetop into the well-watered, well-wooded Morgan Valley below and instantly fell in love.

The year was 1852. Morgan Valley looked like Ohio's green valleys. Later,

Thurston crossed the mountain and camped in the hollow three days. He became determined to live there. Only one obstacle prevented him. Morgan Valley was surrounded by mountains. The rugged canyon where the Weber River flows was the only possible route for wagons.

Three years later, Thurston finally persuaded a friend, two sons and a son-in-law to blaze a road through Weber River Canyon. Shovels, picks, crowbars and a small plow were their tools. Some places in the canyon were so narrow, the men loosened boulders high up and rolled them to the river below. These were used to build a foundation for a road.

In 1993, the highest peak in Davis and Morgan counties was named after this Mormon pioneer. A plaque on the 9,707-foot summit—also the boundary for the two counties—tells his story.

Thurston Peak is directly above Layton and four peaks north of the white-domed Federal Aviation Administration's radar station on Francis Peak near Bountiful. Reaching its summit from the east side is arduous. More than a 4,000-foot elevation gain in about three miles, it also requires crossing private land at the mouth of any canyon access. The waterfall in Adams Canyon is worth a hike, though the trail to Thurston is actually on the north ridge.

The legal route starts at the radar station on Francis Peak and follows the Great Western Trail north for an eight-mile walk to Thurston. The view is worth the exertion. From the summit, Great Salt Lake sprawls across the basin below. On a clear day, many of its deseret islands pock the water. To the east is the lush Morgan Valley. There are the Oquirrh Mountains to the southwest with the Stansbury Mountains peeking over their shoulders. South on the ridgeline is a profile of the Wasatch. North are the jagged peaks near Ogden.

Thurston's rounded summit is some of the oldest rock in Utah—2.5 billion years. It has been manipulated and pushed into a mountain by geologic forces.

"Few localities in the world expose older rocks," said Bill Parry, geology professor at the University of Utah. "They have been through numerous episodes of heating, reheating, burial, exhumation and compression."

These mountains are also world travelers. Imagine the earth as an intact egg with its shell shattered. Some of the shell fragments—called plates by scientists—are covered by ocean. Others hold continents. Plates covered with water dive under each other, while liquid rock fills the cracks left behind. Continents on the other hand are buoyant, always bobbing around on the surface. This way land masses move around.

Thurston Peak, part of the North American plate, was next to East Antarctica 750 million years ago. Later it was the western margin of South America, Africa and eventually Western Europe. Now joined by other ancient rocks, such as those found on the Colorado River in the Grand Canyon and Wyoming's Wind River Mountains, it forms North America's backbone. In more modern times—100 million years ago—Thurston Peak's rocks were compressed, folded, and faulted. The Wasatch fault pushed them upward.

DAVIS AND MORGAN COUNTIES —
THURSTON PEAK

NORTH

△ Thurston Peak

DAVIS COUNTY

MORGAN COUNTY

Kaysville

89

15

Farmington Canyon

Wasatch Range

Ⓟ △ *Francis Peak (has radar towers)*

100 East

Farmington

State Road 227

To Bountiful Peak

Exit 325

Wasatch-Cache National Forest

15

Centerville

Bountiful

LEGEND

▬▬	Major Highway
▬	Asphalt Road
—	Dirt Road
Ⓟ	Car Park
-----	Trail
▬▬▬	Ridgeline, County Line

1 mile

UTAH

Thurston Peak
9,707 ft.

Davis & Morgan Co.

Cross-country skiing is just one of the many recreational activities to be enjoyed on Utah's highest peaks. Paula Huff

Glaciers and running water gave Thurston Peak its shape today.

Straight canyons and the jutting ridgeline created by this erosion makes its weather intense. Eddy winds travel over the ridge, shift directions and become wildly erratic, said Ed Carle, National Weather Service lead forecaster in Salt Lake City. Air moving across Great Salt Lake gathers moisture and dumps powdery snow or rain. Other times wind funneling through the narrow, relatively straight canyons becomes more swift because of the restriction. "We've had up to 100-mile-an-hour winds in those canyons," Carle said.

Humans have watched it all for eons. Various American Indian tribes have migrated through, leaving arrowhead, spear points, broken pottery, grinding stones, and graves still found today. In one of the first written accounts, mountain man Jim Bridger and a group encountered Blackfoot Indians in 1825. Near present-day Farmington, there was a battle with both sides losing men.

Northwest Shoshones were the predominant tribe in the 1850s. They were gatherers and hunters who lived in tepees. Because they were nomadic, they established well-worn trails through these mountains, says William W. Terry, author of *Weber County is Worth Knowing*.

It was the Northwest Shoshone who taught starving Mormons about Utah's edible plants, such as sego lily bulbs. But these early white settlers chose abodes different than their instructors—homes dug out of the north banks of streams. Elias Adams lived in one of these dugouts at the mouth of Adams Canyon, named in his honor. With his sons' help, he built one of the first reservoirs for storing irrigation water in western North America in 1852. Though modernized now, it still exists.

Farming was the only way to survive in the early years of settlement. With irrigation the land grew wheat, oats, corn, potatoes, turnips, squash, cabbage, pumpkins, peas, carrots, and beets.

Grasshoppers were so thick from 1865–1868 that they looked like clouds in the setting sun, according to an account in *East of Antelope Island*. Settlers fought them with fire and flails. Many of the insects dropped into Great Salt Lake and "were washed upon the lake shore like levees for miles in length and smelled terrible..."

"It was quite ordinary then to go into the mountains above this community and bring out a grizzly bear," writes David F. Smith in his book *My Native Village*.

Deer, elk, and moose are the only big game left today.

Logs were eventually carried down from the mountains for homes. The hills were too steep for wagons so each tree was dragged out by horses. Later adobes, rocks, and bricks were used. As these settlers developed their own lifestyle, they still had contact with American Indians.

By 1923, Thurston Peak and the foothills below were denuded by overgrazing and fires. On August 13, a cloudburst pushed walls of water and mud down every canyon. Five boy scouts on a camping trip in a canyon were killed. A couple honeymooning also lost their lives, writes George Quincy Knowlton in *A History of Farmington, Utah*. After a survey, the federal government decided the flood was caused by overuse. Terracing and replanting began.

Today, sheep grazing occurs on these mountains. Mining and timber cutting are history. They mostly provide water and recreation for the population below.

Thirty summer homes are scattered over the Farmington Flats area, along with the Bountiful Peak and Sunset campgrounds. There is also a group reservation site. Besides campers, snowmobilers, mountain bikers, fourwheelers, and hikers are the most common users. For K. Achter that has proven a problem.

When the valley was settled, few right-of-ways were set aside at canyon mouths. On the east side of Thurston Peak, hikers must cross private land for a direct route to the summit. At Adams Canyon where Achter owns 35 acres, recreationists were permitted until the abuse began. People began burning live trees, destroying his sprinkler system and causing erosion by skidding mountain bike tires down steep trails. Now, when he places "no trespassing" signs, the are torn down with a week.

For now, Davis County Planner Barry Burton is working with Achter and other landowners to create a right-of-way. Until then, the only legal access to Thurston Peak is the Great Western Trail going north from the Francis Peak radar stations.

— Paula Huff

Summit:	13,528 ft.
Difficulty:	Difficult.
USGS maps:	Gilbert Peak NE, Mount Powell, Kings Peak.
Length:	11.5 miles using route from Gunsight Pass; 14 miles using the trail.

Trailhead: Drive east on I-80 past Evanston to the Fort Bridger exit. Take Wyoming Highway 414 past Mountain View to Lonetree. Take the first right turn at Lonetree and follow the dirt road, past ranches and oil wells, for 18 miles to the Henrys Fork trailhead. It is eight miles to Dollar Lake and about four hours each way to the top of Kings Peak. The Henrys Fork Trailhead is at an elevation of about 9,400 feet. Dollar Lake is about 10,800 feet and Gunsight Pass is 11,888. Anderson Pass is 12,700 feet in elevation. There is plenty of water in Henrys Fork, although it is necessary to carry a water filter and pack water for the trail in.

Because of the approach length, Kings Peak is moderately difficult. Trail access is good right up to Anderson Pass.

The hike: While herding sheep in the Uinta Mountains in the 1930s, David B. Hall often gazed at the lofty summit of Kings Peak and daydreamed about the day he would climb it.

Hiking the peak at age 79 wasn't necessarily part of that dream. But that's what happened. With three sons, seven grandchildren and South Carolina friends in tow, Hall ascended Utah's highest peak in August 1996.

"I'm planning on climbing Kings next summer, too, just to say I did it at 80," said Hall, who lives in Vernal. "Actually, my entire goal is to climb the three highest peaks in Utah: Kings, Gilbert and Mt. Emmons."

At 13,528 feet, Kings Peak is Duchesne County's highest point. This summit covered with Volkswagon-size rocks is named for Clarence King, who surveyed the 40th parallel so precisely his work is rarely questioned to this day.

A 24-year-old geologist working for the California Geological Survey, King became pressed for money when his step-father died. His salary could not support his mother and her three young children. Perched atop a high peak in the Sierra Nevada, King looked west upon the Great Basin and dreamed. The transcontinental railroad would soon cross this desert barrier to join the East and West coasts. Geology, flora, fauna, potential investment and settlement along the railroad line was a mystery.

King presented his idea to survey the 40th parallel to folks in Washington D.C. By 1867, he had marching orders. Four years later, King had worked his way into the Uinta Mountains, an area he later wrote about as being the "most arduous" surveying in his experience, according to the biography Clarence King by Thurman Wilkins.

DUCHESNE COUNTY — KINGS PEAK

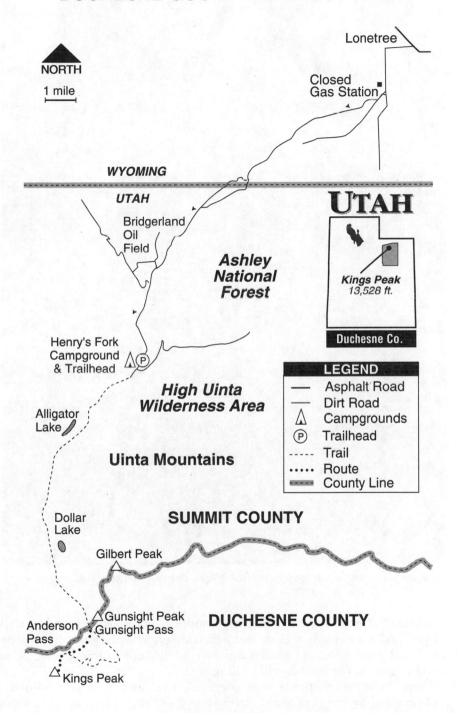

Lonetree

Closed
Gas Station

NORTH

1 mile

WYOMING

UTAH

Bridgerland
Oil
Field

Ashley
National
Forest

UTAH

Kings Peak
13,528 ft.

Duchesne Co.

Henry's Fork
Campground
& Trailhead

High Uinta
Wilderness Area

LEGEND	
—	Asphalt Road
—	Dirt Road
⚠	Campgrounds
Ⓟ	Trailhead
-----	Trail
.....	Route
▬▬▬	County Line

Alligator
Lake

Uinta Mountains

SUMMIT COUNTY

Dollar
Lake

Gilbert Peak

Gunsight Peak
Gunsight Pass

DUCHESNE COUNTY

Anderson
Pass

Kings Peak

A backpacker works his way into Utah's high country. Paula Huff

"Drought, forest fire, canyons, remote supplies of forage...lofty snow-clad ranges, and wide plains regions through which artificial signals have to be used, and most of all, an almost uninterrupted smoky atmosphere, combined to give us constant trouble," King wrote.

Once these high summits were surveyed, King and his troops followed trails created by trappers to get down Henry's Fork, "the haunt of lawless mountain men."

Though King's survey gained him scientific recognition, it is an incident during the work that made him famous. In 1871, prospectors Philip Arnold and John Slack deposited several sacks of rough diamonds in the Bank of California, San Francisco, according to the 1941 edition of *Utah: A Guide to the State*. They told bank president William Ralston about discovering the precious gems 1,000 miles east of San Francisco. After a mining engineer and Southern Pacific Railroad official examined the site, a $10 million company was organized. Then King visited the field, now known as Diamond Gulch, in the Uinta Mountains.

"He found diamonds in tree forks and rock crevices, but none in the underlying rock," according to *Utah: A Guide to the State*. "Finally he uncovered a large diamond bearing stonecutter's marks, showing that the field had been salted....The prospectors got away with $660,000, and Ralston shouldered the loss, hanging the framed receipts on his office wall."

Once a lonely, far-off place, 243,956 acres of the Uinta Mountains were set aside by the US Forest Service in 1931 as a primitive area. Fifty-three years later the name was changed to High Uintas Wilderness Area.

Now, the peak bearing King's moniker, which sits smack-dab in the middle of the wilderness area, attracts more than 10,000 hikers, runners, and skiers annually. In addition, 15 to 25 percent of all visitors use horses.

All the attention makes it difficult for Gayne Sears to provide Kings Peak visitors with a wilderness experience: solitude and a sense of what daily life was like for those who lived in the area hundreds of years before.

"Oftentimes you can see 100 people on the peak each day in July and August," said Sears, wilderness resource coordinator for the south slope of the Uintas out of the Ashley National Forest's Roosevelt office. "The area is highly used and relatively highly impacted as far as campfire rings, live trees cut down for firewood and vegetation missing from around the lakes."

This wasn't always the case. Compared to how American Indians used surrounding mountain ranges, the central Uintas were practically shunned. Knives, pottery, and camp sites left by American Indians roaming the Uintas up to 6,000 years ago can be found. Most of the tribes came from the north. But getting food from the central Uintas required too much effort. Hunting parties had to walk through what archaeologists call a dead zone, a broad belt of woodland that provided few usable resources for humans.

"Because it is so hard to get in and out of these mountains it was actually easier to get most of the food in the lowland areas," said David Madsen, Utah State paleoecologist. "The time spent traveling could be spent gathering food, so when you add it all together it was easier to stay where they were."

About 125 miles long, the Uintas are the largest east-west trending mountain range in the western hemisphere. Rocks visible now are Precambrian sandstone and shale, stones so old that when deposited 600 million years ago, living organisms did not have skeletons, said Andy Godfrey, a geomorphologist for the USDA Forest Service in Ogden. The landscape pushed upward about 70 million years ago, and the land tilted slightly toward the south. Glaciers formed a half million years ago. When the ice melted 10,000 years ago, the land had warped into broad U-shaped valleys.

Father Silvestre Velez de Escalante and Father Francisco Atanasio Dominguez left the first written record of the Uintas. Accompanied by a Spanish soldiers and American Indians, the priests walked along the mountain's southern flank in 1776.

General William H. Ashley, leader of the first trapping expedition to reach present Utah, crossed the Uintas in 1825. Twenty-two year later, a food shortage among Mormon settlers led to the next known record.

Finally prospectors, cowboys, and sheepherders began wandering among the forests and peaks. It was these early explorers who began stocking fish in the high Uinta lakes.

"Sheepherders and prospectors found higher lakes empty of fish, natural barriers preventing the fish from spawning farther up," according to *Utah: A Guide to the State*. "They would catch a few fingerlings in a bucket, carry them up, and empty them in good but unproductive lakes. This method of transplanting fish was the only one used in this area until 1910, when official stocking of rainbow and eastern brook trout was begun."

Now basins at the foot of Kings Peak attract thousands of recreationists who dangle lines in the meandering streams for brook, rainbow and cut-throat trout. Moose, elk, deer, beaver, marmots, ptarmigan, pica, and raptors can also be seen.

And sometimes famous wildlife of the human variety even appear. Sir Edmund Percival Hillary, a New Zealand mountain climber who became one of the first two men to reach the top of Mount Everest and return, is one. In 1978, Steve Schueler spent 10 days backpacking in the Yellowstone drainage that leads to Kings Peak. While there he stumbled upon a large encampment with a huge variety of tents. Top executives from Sears Roebuck and Sears Canada had converged to test camping gear. Along was Hillary, who represented their line of equipment.

"So here were these overstressed, urban-type guys who smoked and drank too much, and they were at 10,000 feet trying to hike with Sir Edmund Hillary," Schueler recalled. "He was marching around the hills easily, leaving these much younger men in the dust. We passed one guy who was trying to get up to Bluebell Pass. He was smoking a cigarette while trying to catch his breath."

The evening before Hillary and entourage left, Schueler was invited into the encampment for dinner.

"They had taken everything in by horse, and they had ice boxes, a complete bar with all kinds of alcohol and this incredible array of food," Schueler recalled. "We had lobster thermidor. I remember eating this incredible food, then sitting around the campfire. Everybody had their Sierra Club cups, and they were sipping this expensive brandy, talking about what Hillary was up to."

Hillary is a "quirky" person, recalls Schueler. Physically, he is large and he had "a good size paunch going, but was still fit and outdoors looking."

— *Paula Huff*

8 EMERY AND SANPETE COUNTIES — TWO WASATCH PLATEAU PEAKS (EAST MOUNTAIN AND SOUTH TENT MOUNTAIN)

East Mountain

Summit:	10,743 ft.
Difficulty:	Easy.
USGS map:	Rilda Canyon.
Length:	1 mile.

South Tent Mountain

Summit:	11,285 ft.
Difficulty:	Easy.
USGS map:	South Tent Mountain, Spring City.
Length:	1.75 miles.

East Mountain

Trailhead: From Joe's Valley Reservoir Marina, drive north along the west side of the reservoir. After one mile, turn right at the stop sign. Continue north. The road veers west, then turns south. As it turns south, look for a road to the left with a sign that says Huntington Canyon and Upper Joe's Valley. Turn left onto this dirt road. After 3 miles, the road comes to an intersection with a sign. Turn toward Upper Joe's Valley. After 5 miles, you reach another intersection and sign. Turn right toward Indian Creek and Cottonwood Canyon. After about a mile, there is another intersection with a sign. Turn left toward Indian Creek. Drive 2 miles to the Indian Creek Campground and turn right onto the Spoon Creek Road. Drive about two miles until you reach a fence and cattle guard. East Mountain is the peak on the north side of the fence. Notice the treeless area near the top. There is no trail. Head toward it by first following the fence up the drainage, then climbing the steep open area to the peak. Expect to hike over some deadfall in a thick forest. A geologic survey marker is found near the top of the peak. For those who don't want to hike, there are two roads in the area which allow visitors to drive to near the top of the peak.

South Tent Mountain

Trailhead: From the Sanpete County hamlet of Spring City, turn left at a sign that says Spring City Canyon. (Listed as Oak Creek on some maps.) The road is dirt. Soon you will come to a Y intersection. Stay left. After about 5 miles, you come to a T intersection. Turn left again. The right fork goes to a picnic area. After seven miles, you reach the top of the Wasatch Plateau and another intersection. Turn right onto the Skyline Drive road. After three miles, there is a sign that reads: "South Tent Mountain. 11,282 elevation." A road to the left goes to the top of North Tent Mountain. If driving a two-wheel drive vehicle, park and begin walking. Or, drive the rough four-wheel

EAST MOUNTAIN — EMERY COUNTY

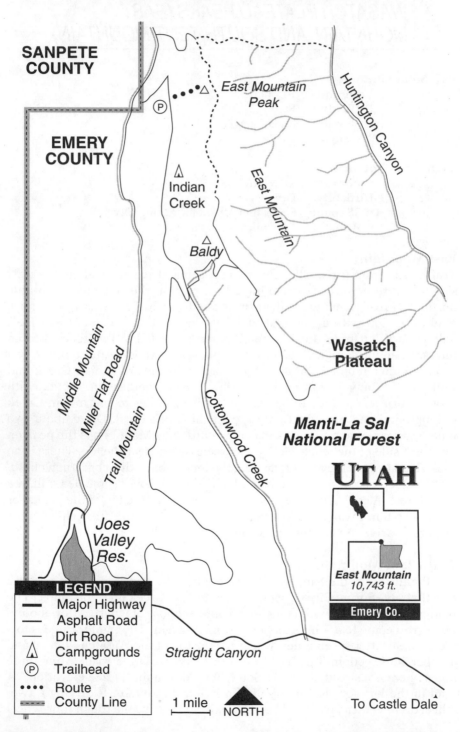

SANPETE COUNTY

EMERY COUNTY

East Mountain Peak

Huntington Canyon

Indian Creek

East Mountain

Baldy

Middle Mountain

Miller Flat Road

Trail Mountain

Cottonwood Creek

Wasatch Plateau

Manti-La Sal National Forest

UTAH

East Mountain
10,743 ft.

Emery Co.

Joes Valley Res.

LEGEND
—	Major Highway
—	Asphalt Road
—	Dirt Road
△	Campgrounds
℗	Trailhead
••••	Route
– – –	County Line

Straight Canyon

1 mile

NORTH

To Castle Dale

SOUTH TENT MOUNTAIN — SANPETE COUNTY

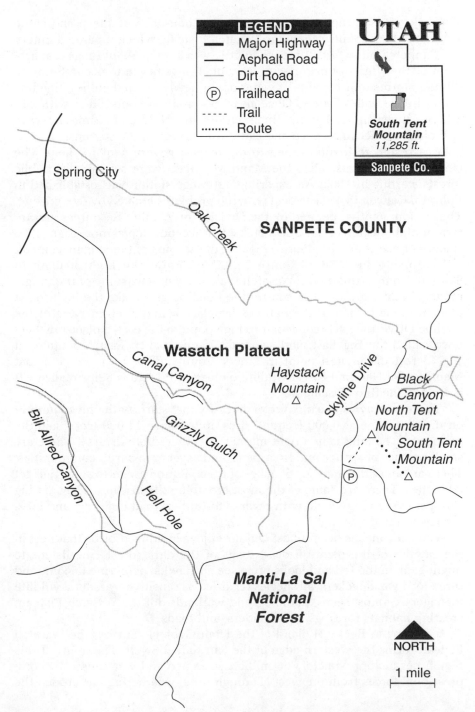

LEGEND
— Major Highway
— Asphalt Road
— Dirt Road
Ⓟ Trailhead
----- Trail
.... Route

UTAH

South Tent Mountain
11,285 ft.

Sanpete Co.

Spring City

Oak Creek

SANPETE COUNTY

Wasatch Plateau

Canal Canyon

Haystack Mountain △

Skyline Drive

Black Canyon

North Tent Mountain △

South Tent Mountain △

Bill Allred Canyon

Grizzly Gulch

Hell Hole

Ⓟ

Manti-La Sal National Forest

▲ NORTH

1 mile

drive road to the ridge line. Once on the ridge, follow it in an east by southeast direction down to a saddle, then up to South Tent Mountain. There is a faint trail. A geological-survey marker is found at the top of the peak.

The hike: It was the turn of the century. Thousands of sheep and cattle grazed the high country along the Wasatch Plateau, which separated Emery and Sanpete County. At a time when little was known about range management or the effects of overgrazing, terrible things began to occur. Summer thunderstorms sent torrents of water down newly created gullies, flooding towns in the valley below. Once-clear mountain streams filled with silt, killing native fish. And, in the small settlements, children became sick with typhoid fever because sheep and cattle were dying in the streams.

As a result, residents turned to the federal government for help. The lands on what locals called the Manti Mountain were set aside as public forests starting in 1903. An experimental range station was established in Ephraim Canyon in 1911 to deal with the problems created by overgrazing. The station, jointly operated by the Division of Wildlife Resources and Intermountain Region of the USDA Forest Service, developed more than 1,000 species of plants and has helped pioneer the science of range management.

Visitors to 11,285-foot South Tent Mountain, the highest peak in Sanpete County and on the Wasatch Plateau, can view some of the range-management work done to control the flooding and make the high forest plateau home to one of the nation's largest elk herds. From parts of the Skyline Drive, they also can look to a high point in the east, a place ranchers once called the Big East, and see what is now called East Mountain, at 10,743 feet the highest point in Emery County. This is the domain that Manti-La Sal National Forest wildlife biologist Jill Dufour helps manage. It is a place she finds fascinating.

"There is an awesome mixture of diversity that starts with pinyon juniper on the sandstone at 6,000 feet and rises up to above 11,000 feet," said the biologist. "The land is in a tight mosaic. It is incredibly diverse. There are small patches of spruce and fir, aspens, and sagebrush-shrub communities. There are areas that may get 6 inches of precipitation a year to areas that get 30 inches. There are some of the most erodible soils in Utah. They are big slumps. Everything we do with regards to timber, road building, and grazing has to recognize that."

When she makes her rounds, Dufour enjoys looking at birds that nest in the cavities of the plentiful dead snags of the dark forest. She listens to bugling elk in the fall and looks up to see goshawks, peregrine falcons, and three-toed woodpeckers, all species regarded as sensitive by federal wildlife managers. Sumps, seeps, potholes, and wetlands dot the Wasatch Plateau, creating habitats for frogs, salamanders, and toads.

According to Becky Hylland of the Utah Geologic Survey, the Wasatch Plateau forms the western edge of the San Rafael Swell. The uplift of this region began approximately 66 million years ago and was caused by compressional forces from the west. Through time, weathering has eroded the

East Mountain, Emery County's highest peak, is covered with sandstone boulders. Paula Huff

San Rafael portion, which was once topographically higher than the Wasatch Plateau-Book Cliffs area, leaving behind the Wasatch Plateau, an area rich with coal, oil, and gas resources.

Stan McDonald, a USDA Forest Service archaeologist, said human history on the Wasatch Plateau dates back 9,000 years, with most of the use thought to be seasonal due to the frigid and cold winters in the area. Paleontologists have discovered two mastodons and a mammoth preserved in the rich soils of the mountain in recent years.

The area began to open up even more in the 1930s when crews from the Civilian Conservation Corps and Work Project Administration finished construction on the Skyline Drive, a 100-mile dirt road that runs across the top of the Wasatch Plateau from Salina Canyon on the south to the Tucker rest stop in Spanish Fork Canyon on the north.

"The drive winds along the summit at elevations of 9,000 to 11,000 feet, skirting glacial basins and deep canyons, passing through aspen and evergreen groves and grassy meadows that flaunt displays of wildflowers in late spring and summer," wrote the late Ward Roylance in his guide to Utah. "The full length is open only from July to early October."

Because of the lush grasslands in the mountains, Sanpete County was among the first areas in Utah settled by Mormon pioneers. Roylance wrote that Spring City, once called Allred's Settlement after James Allred, a bodyguard of LDS Church leader Joseph Smith, was first settled in the 1850s but abandoned until the 1860s due to problems with Indians. Some old log barns and homes, many dating to the 1800s, remain, making the town one of the state's most scenic.

When locals headed to the mountain, they couldn't help but notice South Tent Mountain, 12 miles southeast of the city. According to the book *Utah Place Names*, the peak got its name because it was shaped like an old-fashioned tent.

To the east stood another tall mountain in Emery County. Montell Seely, a Castle Dale rancher who owns 3,000 acres of land on East Mountain, knows the area's history well. He should. Each year, he organizes the Castle Valley pageant in late July and early August that celebrates the history of Emery County. Seely also takes groups on handcart trips across the mountain, camping near the summit of East Mountain.

Seely said the first trail into the mountain was cut by Tom Hudson in the 1880s. Another trail, in Roan's Canyon, was built a few years later. In 1959, working with officials of what was then known as the Church Mine, Seely joined Fred Cox and Fred Van Buren of Orangeville in building a new trail.

"I wanted to have an easier access to the mountain, so I got together with Shirl McArthur, the superintendent for the Church Mine operation," he recalled. "The church was piping water to its mine operation from Burnt Tree Spring. It was always a hassle for them to send men to climb the mountain to fix the water line. And it was a hassle for the livestock men to take cattle up Tom's Trail or to drive all the way around Mill Canyon to get on East Mountain with a vehicle."

Many vistas of the Wasatch Plateau can be seen from South Tent Mountain, Sanpete County. Paula Huff

Seely donated his time. The Church Mine provided Cox, Fred Van Buren, a compressor and jackhammer, a bulldozer, and all the dynamite needed to build the road. Seely didn't bother with formal surveying equipment. He simply eyeballed the route of the dugway and marked the route with ribbon.

"I must have walked back and forth and up and down at least six times," he said. "It took 2 tons of dynamite to get the road built and it took us about a month to complete the job. Locals still use the road as a cattle trail. Since the church sold the mine to Utah Power and Light, the company no longer had a need for the water line, so it discontinued maintaining the road for vehicle use."

The forest service kicked sheep off the mountain; they were replaced by cattle and a growing wild elk population. Visitors can drive to near the top of the mountain on two roads, which Seely said can usually be negotiated by two-wheel-drive vehicles with high clearance.

Longtime Emery County resident Tracy Jeffs enjoys being top of the Wasatch Plateau, either on the Skyline Drive, South Tent Mountain or East Mountain.

"You look down on the Sanpete side at those checkerboard areas that are so vivid," he said. "And it's beautiful to look out on the desert to the east."

—Tom Wharton
(Paula Huff also contributed to this story)

9 GARFIELD COUNTY — MT. ELLEN

Summit:	11,522 ft.
Difficulty:	Easy.
USGS map:	Mt. Ellen.
Length:	2.5 miles.

Trailhead: The trail, though not marked, begins at an obvious parking area at the top of 10,485-foot Bull Creek Pass in the Henry Mountains. The most difficult part may be reaching the trailhead on a steep, 56-mile dirt road that almost requires a good four-wheel-drive vehicle. Though there is access on the west side of the Henry Mountains—which makes for a nice loop drive— the easiest way to reach the road to the trailhead is to drive 20.5 miles south of Hanksville on Utah 95 and west on a dirt road. Pick up a free Bureau of Land Management Bull Creek Pass National Back Country Byway brochure in Hanksville or the state office in Salt Lake City for a map and interpretive information.

The hike: An aura of mystery permeates the Henry Mountains, the last mountain range in the 48 contiguous states to be named.

Prospectors once searched for a cursed lost Spanish gold mine, many losing their health, minds, and lives in the process. The Eagle City ghost town, symbolizing the dashed dreams of 1890 gold miners, sits at the base of the mountain, lost and abandoned. Butch Cassidy and his gang of out- laws hid in this wild, roadless country known as Robber's Roost at the turn of the century. And one of the nation's only free-roaming buffalo herds has wandered the range since 1941, when 18 head were transplanted from Yellowstone National Park.

At the top of the range sits 11,522-foot Mt. Ellen, the tallest peak in Garfield County. The boulder-strewn summit—listed in some literature as being 11,615 feet high—sits on the north end of the desert range.

Scott Durfey, a longtime resident of Loa, knows the range well. His par- ents built a cabin on a homestead about one mile west of the summit in 1927, hauling a 450-pound cookstove on the back of a mule. His grandfather owned the Notom Ranch to the east of the peak and, at one time, knew the outlaw Butch Cassidy and some of his gang. Durfey's grandfather, George, told him this story:

"Ed Thomas, who rode with Butch Cassidy, came by the ranch one day and said he was hungry," Durfey recalls. "My grandmother said she'd planned to fix chicken and dumplings but hadn't had time to kill the chickens. Tho- mas asked her how many she needed. She told him four or five. He stepped outside and, cocking his rifle as fast as he could and shooting from the hip, he shot the heads off five chickens."

Another time, the family purchased 200 cows and let them graze on the Henry Mountains during the winter. When spring came, Durfey's grandfa-

GARFIELD COUNTY — MT. ELLEN

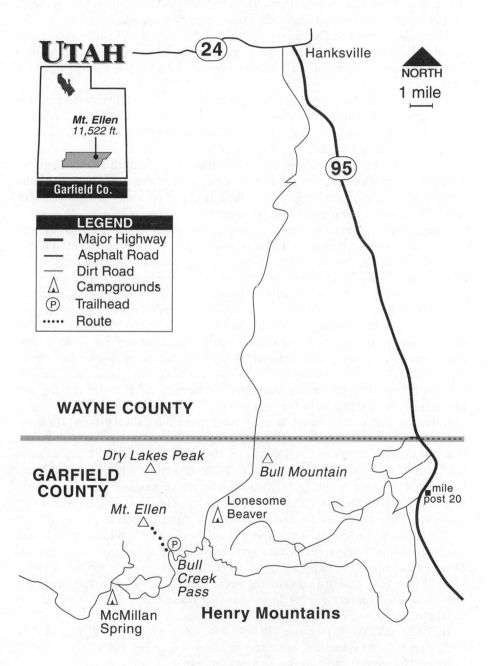

UTAH

Mt. Ellen
11,522 ft.

Garfield Co.

NORTH

1 mile

24

Hanksville

95

LEGEND
— Major Highway
— Asphalt Road
— Dirt Road
⛺ Campgrounds
Ⓟ Trailhead
····· Route

WAYNE COUNTY

Dry Lakes Peak

**GARFIELD
COUNTY**

Bull Mountain

Mt. Ellen

Lonesome
Beaver

■ mile
post 20

*Bull
Creek
Pass*

Henry Mountains

McMillan
Spring

Ragged Mountain

49

ther went looking for the cattle and followed them to the Colorado River. Across the river, he was greeted with a sign from the rustlers who had stolen the animals. It read: "If you value your life, don't come any farther." The group turned around and rode home, empty handed.

Then there was the Depression year of 1932, when the rattlesnakes got so thick that they would bite a horse as it walked through the mountains. That lasted only one year, and no one ever knew why the snakes were so thick.

Perhaps the snake infestation had something to do with the curse of the legendary lost Spanish gold mine, thought to be somewhere near Mount Pennell to the south. B.J. Silliman, in an essay called "Legends, Traditions and Early History of the Henry Mountains," wrote about the curse. As legend has it, an Indian was hired as a cattle hand by one of the early settlers. Around a campfire one night, the native pointed to the mountain and said there was plenty of gold up there. When pressed to show the settlers the spot, he declined, telling the following story:

"Many, many years ago, the Spaniards dug gold out of the side of this mountain. They employed the Indians to do the hard work and treated them shamefully. They were forced to labor from dawn until darkness and were often beaten and kicked like dogs. One morning, the surrounding hills were full of warriors. A terrible battle followed, lasting all day. Many Indians were killed but, in the end, all the Spaniards were destroyed, their shelters burned and their workings carefully filled with all signs obliterated. As the workings were being filled, the Indian medicine man placed a curse on the place from which the gold had been taken. To him who reopened the workings would come great calamity. His blood would turn to water and even in his youth he would be an old man. His wives and children would die and the earth would bring forth for him only poison weed instead of corn."

Silliman then told of many miners who met their fate trying to find the mine. One of those may have been a Maine settler named Edwin Thatcher Wolverton, who came to the Henrys in 1902. Wolverton and his two sons built a mill to crush gold ore in about 1921. But the mill, which has been reconstructed next to the BLM's Hanksville office and can be seen to this day, operated only a short time. An anonymous BLM researcher, writing in an interpretive brochure for the mill, offered this speculation:

"Perhaps the superstitious Wolverton believed an old Indian curse about hardship and suffering resulting from reopening the old gold diggings on Mount Pennell, or perhaps the gold played out, but, whatever the reason, we do know that gold ore was run through the mill for only a short time. We don't know if Wolverton ever found his lost mine but, once in a while, he would come to town with a little gold."

In 1929, E.T. Wolverton died in a Fruita, Colorado, hospital. Wolverton had been injured when he was thrown from a spooked horse and needed surgery. He recovered from the surgery, but died of pneumonia.

Another kind of miner opened this land in the early 1950s. That's when the uranium boom hit southeastern Utah and prospectors went out in all

The Hike to Mt. Ellen, Garfield County's highest peak, gives one an overview of the Colorado Plateau. Tom Wharton

directions, building many dirt roads. Hikers looking to scale Mt. Ellen can take what is now a Bureau of Land Management Back Country Byway to reach the trailhead.

A brochure available at the State Office of the BLM in Salt Lake City or in Hanksville offers a good map and interpretive information on the 56-mile road, which begins 21 miles south of Hanksville off Utah Highway 95 and ends on Utah Highway 276, five miles south of its junction with Utah Highway 95 near the east entrance to Capitol Reef National Park.

The five-mile round-trip hike to the summit is relatively easy, requiring an elevation gain of only 1,037 feet. But the road to 10,485-foot Bull Creek Pass is steep and difficult. A four-wheel-drive vehicle is recommended, though a two-wheel-drive truck with high clearance probably could make the trip.

The entire road is open most years from early July until the snow flies in late October or early November. The Lonesome Beaver Campground on the east slope and McMillan Springs Campground on the west slope are pretty and relatively uncrowded. Both offer drinking water.

The hike to the summit begins at an obvious parking area at Bull Creek Pass. There are a few large pine trees, but most of the hike takes place above timberline over piles of boulders. An obvious trail leads to the two highest points.

Mt. Ellen is the largest laccolithic dome in the Henry Mountains. A laccolithic dome occurs when molten rock pushes its way upward, in this case under the sandstone, without coming to the surface in the form of a volcano. The strewn boulders on top of Mt. Ellen are of the intrusive igneous variety called diorite porphyry, according to Sandy Eldredge of the Utah Geological Survey office. Freezing and thawing action created the piled-up boulders.

From the ridgeline, there are views of the Dirty Devil River, La Sal and Abajo mountains, and Canyonlands country carved by the Colorado River to the east. Navajo Mountain is plainly visible on the south. The Boulder Mountain, Waterpocket Fold, and Capitol Reef National Park are visible on the West.

Mt. Ellen was named after the wife of Almon Thompson and the sister of explorer John Wesley Powell, the first man to chart this remote country, starting in 1869. Thompson was second in command for the government survey Powell conducted in the area.

Powell named the Henry Mountains after Joseph Henry, a physicist who served as secretary of the Smithsonian Institution and who actively supported Powell's Colorado expeditions.

—*Tom Wharton*

10 GRAND AND SAN JUAN COUNTIES—TWO LA SAL MOUNTAINS PEAKS (MT. WAAS AND MT. PEALE)

Mt. Waas

Summit:	12,331 ft.
Difficulty:	Moderate to difficult.
USGS maps:	Warner Lake, Mount Waas.
Length:	3.5 miles.

Mt. Peale

Summit:	12,721 ft.
Difficulty:	Moderate.
USGS map:	Mount Peale, Mount Tukuhnukivatz.
Length:	2.25 miles.

Mt. Waas
Trailhead: From Moab, drive south on Highway 191 to the La Sal Mountain Loop Road sign. Turn onto this asphalt-dirt road and drive 4 miles until reaching a Geyser Pass, Oowah Lake, and Warner Lake sign. Turn in the direction of Oowah and Warner lakes. Follow this road—about 15 miles— until reaching a Miners Basin sign. Turn right onto the rough, dirt Miners Basin road, and drive to Miners Basin Lake. Park and begin hiking along a faint two-track on the north side of the lake until it intersects the main dirt road. Turn right onto this road. After a while it passes a locked gate and comes to a fork. Take the left fork. Walk about 100 yards to another fork. Take the left fork, which has a faint trail. This follows a bulldozer scar that has been furrowed and seeded. While climbing, notice the bottom of Miners Basin to the left, which is covered with avalanche debris. Near the head

MT. WAAS—GRAND COUNTY

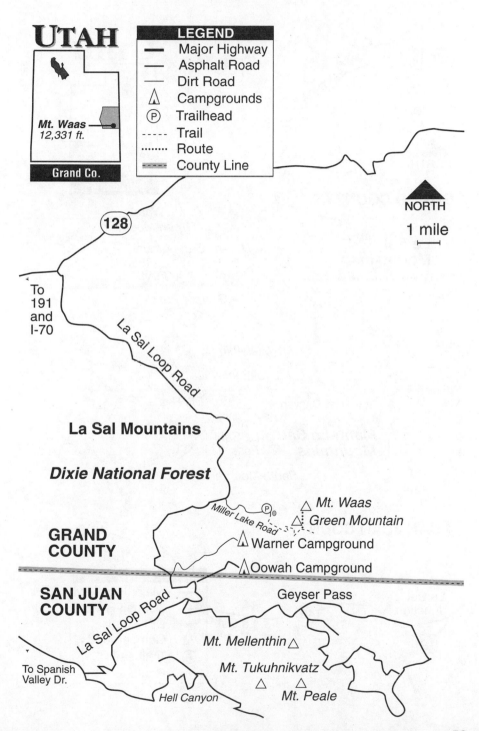

UTAH

Mt. Waas
12,331 ft.

Grand Co.

LEGEND
— Major Highway
— Asphalt Road
— Dirt Road
△ Campgrounds
Ⓟ Trailhead
----- Trail
······· Route
▦▦▦ County Line

NORTH

1 mile

128

To
191
and
I-70

La Sal Loop Road

La Sal Mountains

Dixie National Forest

Miller Lake Road

Ⓟ

△ Mt. Waas
△ Green Mountain

GRAND COUNTY

△ Warner Campground

△ Oowah Campground

SAN JUAN COUNTY

La Sal Loop Road

Geyser Pass

Mt. Mellenthin △

To Spanish
Valley Dr.

Mt. Tukuhnikvatz

△

Hell Canyon

△ Mt. Peale

MT. PEALE—SAN JUAN COUNTY

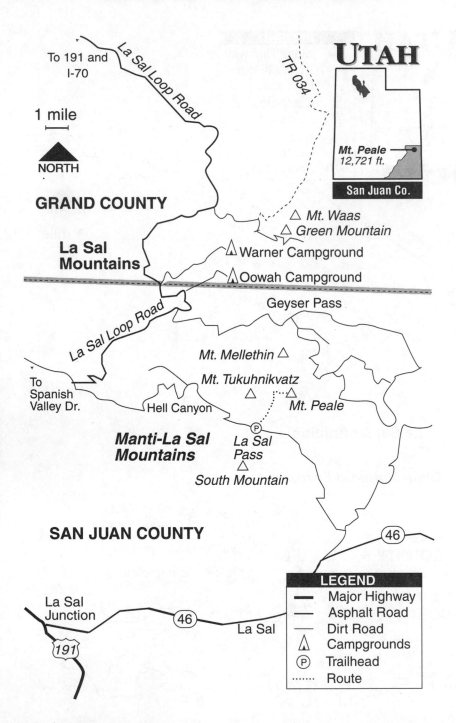

To 191 and I-70

La Sal Loop Road

TR 034

1 mile

NORTH

UTAH

Mt. Peale
12,721 ft.

San Juan Co.

GRAND COUNTY

△ Mt. Waas
△ Green Mountain

La Sal Mountains

⛺ Warner Campground

⛺ Oowah Campground

Geyser Pass

La Sal Loop Road

Mt. Mellethin △

To Spanish Valley Dr.

Mt. Tukuhnikvatz

Hell Canyon

△   △ Mt. Peale

Ⓟ

Manti-La Sal Mountains

La Sal Pass

△
South Mountain

SAN JUAN COUNTY

46

La Sal Junction

46

La Sal

191

LEGEND
▬▬	Major Highway
—	Asphalt Road
—	Dirt Road
△	Campgrounds
Ⓟ	Trailhead
······	Route

of the basin turn left. Follow a long switchback, then turn right onto another switchback that contours east. After following another set of switchbacks to the left and right, there is a fork. Take the switchback to the left. After walking a short distance there is another fork. Take the switchback to the right. From here follow switchbacks to the ridge, being careful to avoid deadends. On the ridgeline, Pilot Mountain is toward the right and Green Mountain, with an electronic relay installation on its summit, is left. Follow the ridgeline over Green Mountain, continuing north to Mt. Waas. Follow switchbacks on Mount Waas's talus slopes for easier walking.

Mt. Peale
Trailhead: From Moab, drive about 20 miles south on Highway 191. At La Sal Junction—or State Route 46—turn east. Drive 12.5 miles until seeing a major dirt road angling off to the left. Turn onto this good two-wheel road, following the signs to La Sal Pass, about 11 miles. At the pass, face north. Mt. Peale is the rounded peak to the right. Mt. Tukuhnikivatz is the more pointed peak to the left. There is no trail to Mt. Peale. Route-find across a meadow, then through aspen and evergreen trees to a talus drainage on the west side of Mt. Peale. This drainage can be seen from La Sal Pass. Walk up the drainage to the ridge. Turn right and follow the ridgeline to Mt. Peale, being careful when crossing its steep talus slopes.

The hikes: The La Sal Mountains house San Juan County's highest peak, Mt. Peale at 12,721 feet, and Grand County's highest peak, Mt. Waas at

The ridgeline leading to Mt. Peale, San Juan County's highest peak, is covered with loose, easy moving talus.. Paula Huff

12,331 feet. When gold fever swept across the United States in the mid-1800s, people flocked to this southeastern edge of Utah, where five towns, at 10,000 feet, were thrown together by folks searching for the sparkling precious metal.

Miners Basin had a general store, livery stable, two restaurants, two saloons, a sheriff's office and 10,000 residents, said Jose Knighton, author of *La Sal Mountains: Hiking and Nature Handbook*. Just over a 12,000-foot ridge in Bachelor Basin lived 300 unmarried men and not a single woman—hence the name. Many claimed Schuman Gulch, Gold Basin, and Lackey Basin as base camp, too. When these high-country residents laid down picks and shovels, they socialized in other camps by traveling a path running the length of the range that connected the towns—now called the Trans La Sal Trail.

"They were great partyers," said Sam Taylor, a third-generation Moab resident and co-editor/publisher of the town's *Times-Independent* newspaper. "I remember my parents' peers talking about hiking over [a 12,000-foot] pass and down into Miners Basin for a dance. They would drink and dance all night, then walk back over the pass to get home."

Time has reduced those boisterous towns to scattered debris and stories told by grandchildren. Livestock and timber provided more viable incomes, and still do today. But the high peaks, mountain lakes, and a respite from the surrounding desert heat still draw many.

From the tip-top, red rocks of the contorted Colorado Plateau stretch to the south and west horizons. To the east is Colorado's Uncompahgre Plateau and the 14,000-foot San Juan Mountains. Underfoot is talus, talus, and more talus.

Magma flowing upward from deep within the Earth created a massive bulge about 24 million years ago, later to become La Sal Mountain. Rather than breaking through the surface, the liquid rock wedged into sedimentary layers and remained underneath where it gradually cooled. The formation is called a laccolith. Erosion later exposed the laccolith. The stone—called diorite—began fracturing and eroding into the talus slopes seen today. With this falling, shifting debris came rock glaciers, a phenomenon visible in few Utah mountain ranges. The La Sals happen to be one.

Talus—a pile of rock debris at the base of a cliff—has a lot of pore spaces that marmots and pikas call home. These openings also allow dense, cold air to sink inward, displacing warmer oxygen. Air at the heart of these stone piles is freezing, so any water solidifies and the pore spaces become choked with ice.

"Pretty soon these rocks are cemented together and the ice-rock mixture begins moving like a glacier," said Don Currey, University of Utah geography professor. "In the upper few feet, you don't see the ice, but lower down it is there."

These rock glaciers often start at the base of a cliff. They look like lobes moving away from the steep face, making the landscape ripple with ridges and furrows. Another sure sign of a rock glacier is an extremely cold stream seeping out of the downhill tip.

Mt. Wass, Grand County's highest peak, looks like an arduous hike from this vantage point. But a switchback trail in the talus makes the trip easier walking. Paula Huff

"There are at least a dozen rock glaciers in the La Sals," Currey said. "The next best place to see one is Wheeler Peak Cirque [in Nevada's Great Basin National Park]."

Other rock glaciers in Utah can be seen in Snowbird's Gad Valley near the base of American Fork Twin Peaks; around Red Castle Lake in the Uintas; and above Emerald Lake off Timpanogos Peak. Little is known about the earliest human inhabitants who may have seen these rock glaciers 7,000 years ago.

"In these people's struggle for survival in a desert landscape, the La Sals offered a seasonal escape from the fierce summer sun," wrote Knighton in *La Sal Mountains*. "As winter snow retreated upslope, the hunter-gatherers climbed gradually heavenward tracking bighorn sheep, deer, elk and bear They collected berries, acorns and other valuable plants as the harvest matured."

Fremont and Anasazi who moved into lowlands surrounding the La Sals 1,500 years ago probably used the mountains in the same way. But they left more evidence of their passing—rock art and dwellings still seen today.

But a different cultures' name for the mountain is used today. La Sal is Spanish for "the salt." The 1776 Dominguez and Escalante expedition said the peaks were named "because close to it there are salt beds where . . . the Yutas [Utes] who live hereabouts get their salt."

Many summit names date from the 1875 Hayden Survey. James L. Gardner and Henry Gannett led the team that mapped the United States' newest territory and some of its least-known country. Mt. Peale was named after Albert Peale, the Hayden Survey's mineralogist. An American Indian guide for the group had his name attached to Mount Waas.

Other names give a peek into the region's past. Mt. Tukuhnikivats is Ute for "where the sun sets last." And Mt. Mellenthin was named after Rudolf Mellenthin. A Moab forest ranger, Mellenthin was a German immigrant who favored silk scarves, high boots, big guns and strutting horses, wrote Knighton. On August, 23, 1918, he was killed in the La Sal Mountains by a World War I draft dodger. As a tribute, the second highest peak was named after him.

Many areas carry the name of families who graze cattle there, such as Taylor Flats, named for Sam Taylor's ancestors. But Taylor's clan has been out of the cattle business for three generations. To him, the La Sals offer a temporary relief from the desert's summer heat. Sometimes a little adventure gets mixed in, especially since the peaks harbor one of the largest black bear populations in Utah.

"I was hiking down a basin one day and came face to face with the cutest little bear cub I'd ever seen," Taylor said. "Then I heard its angry ma behind me, and I swear I walked backwards up a cliff."

— Paula Huff

11 IRON COUNTY — BRIAN HEAD PEAK

Summit:	11,307.
Difficulty:	Easy.
USGS map:	Brian Head.
Length:	Drive to within 100 feet of the top in summer; 3-mile ski in winter.

Trailhead: To reach Brian Head Peak, drive south through the town of Brian Head on State Highway 143 to a well-marked turnoff 0.6 mile south of the north entrance of Cedar Breaks National Monument. The sign may be buried during years of heavy snowfall. In summer, it's possible to drive within a few hundred feet of the top. In winter, skiers and snowmobiles can follow the road three miles.

The hike: Bill Murphy can only smile when perched on the top of 11,307-foot Brian Head Peak, the highest point in Iron County. On a windy, wintry day, he forgets the problems of running two businesses or his duties as a member of the Brian Head City Council, assistant fire chief, state trails council member, and head of the town's search and rescue squad.

Instead, he looks out at Nevada's Wheeler and Highland peaks, Arizona's Mount Trumbull and Navajo Mountain, Beaver County's Tushar Range and

Signs of the state's early history can be found on many of Utah's high peaks.
Paula Huff

the Paunsagunt, Table Cliffs, and Aquarius plateaus. Then, turning west, Murphy looks at little-known ranges with mysterious names such as the Never Summer Mountains and the Wah Wahs and starts to dream.

"I look at those west desert peaks," he said, "and know there are lots of peaks that have never been skied. They are still available for me to explore."

Murphy laughs when asked about how Brian Head Peak got its name. It seems there are three stories.

Bryan to Brian? One story has it that the peak was known as Monument Point until the 1920s. A local resident thought the peak's south-facing side resembled the profile of William Jennings Bryan, a former presidential candidate and one of the lawyers in the Scopes Monkey Trial. Her idea to change the name was accepted by the USDA Forest Service, which misspelled the name.

Another local legend says the peak was named for one of John Wesley Powell's surveyors. Still another says it is named after a local sheepherder. One thing seems certain. The peak has served human needs for thousands of years.

"There is evidence of quite a bit of American Indian activity," said Marian Jacklin, Dixie National Forest archaeologist. "They used Brian Head churt to make stone tools. And they lived there 8,000 years ago in the summer months."

On Jan. 4, 1898, a group of pioneers intent on getting wood to construct the first building at a college that was then known as the Branch Normal School but would eventually become Cedar City's Southern Utah University organized an expedition to an area just below the peak. They were told by state officials that if the building wasn't built that year, they would lose the school.

Heber Jensen operated a sawmill about 10 miles east of the peak. Evidence of the old road can still be seen cut right under Brian Head Peak near what is now the Brian Head ski area. The group had to switch from wagons to sleighs due to deep snow. After reaching the mill, the workers got hit by a huge snowstorm on January 8 and were forced to camp five miles southwest of the peak on January 9. That's when an old sorrel horse came to the rescue. As the story goes, the horse had fallen into a canyon filled with snow as a young colt. The boy who owned it gave it up for dead, but the horse worked his way back up. Now, remembering those skills, the sorrel saved the group by pulling the sleds through the big drifts, getting them to some old cabins at a place called Old Setting. When a new group of settlers joined the group on January 9 with fresh supplies, the mission was successfully completed, the building constructed and the budding college saved.

The building, Old Main, sits west of the Shakespearean Theater to this day. A monument to the old sorrel horse was constructed near Southern Utah University's Centrum athletic stadium.

Steve Heath, a professor of math at the university for the past 27 years, says his son's Boy Scout troop is constructing eight historical markers along

IRON COUNTY — BRIAN HEAD PEAK

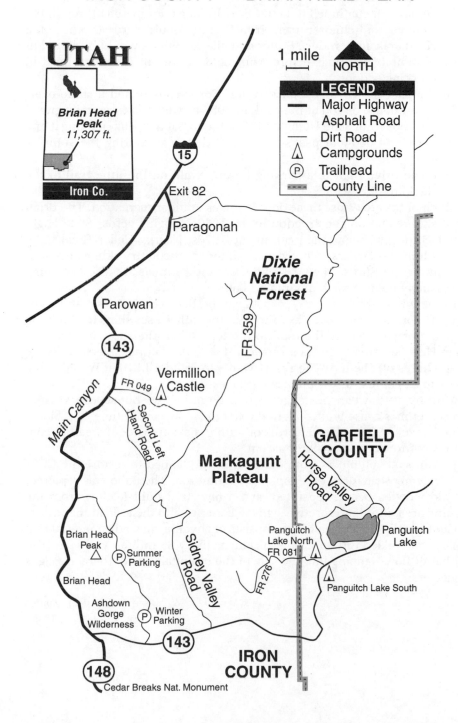

UTAH

Brian Head Peak
11,307 ft.

Iron Co.

1 mile

NORTH

LEGEND
Major Highway
Asphalt Road
Dirt Road
△ Campgrounds
Ⓟ Trailhead
County Line

15

Exit 82

Paragonah

Dixie National Forest

Parowan

FR 359

143

Main Canyon

FR 049

Vermillion △ Castle

Second Left Hand Road

Markagunt Plateau

GARFIELD COUNTY

Horse Valley Road

Panguitch Lake North
FR 081

Panguitch Lake

Brian Head Peak
△
Ⓟ Summer Parking

Sidney Valley Road

FR 276

△

Brian Head

Ashdown Gorge Wilderness
Ⓟ Winter Parking

△ Panguitch Lake South

143

148

IRON COUNTY

Cedar Breaks Nat. Monument

the 28-mile Old Sorrel Trail. The Dixie National Forest will make the old route an official trail.

The mountain continued to be used by humans. From 1904 through the 1920s, women and children from Iron County would herd cows into the Brian Head area and produce butter and cheese, which would be stored in the cool mountain springs before being sold in the fall. The men lived in town, working odd jobs.

Jacklin said the Civilian Conservation Corps constructed a stone over-look and outhouse on top of the peak in 1937 as well as a three-mile gravel road that leads from State Highway 143 to the top of the peak, making it one of the easier 11,000-foot peaks in the world to scale during the summer months.

"You can drive right to a parking lot and walk on the little trail to the vista," Jacklin said.

Much of the area's use these days involves outdoor recreation. The Brian Head ski area began construction in the 1960s, moving across State High-way 143 to right below the peak in the 1970s. Nearby Cedar Breaks National Monument offers scenic vistas, winter cross-country skiing and summer hiking to visitors. The peak and surrounding areas are also becoming increasingly popular with mountain bikers.

In the winter, the wind-swept vista can be reached by snowmobilers or by cross-country skiers such as Murphy, who either uses skins to climb the ridgeline or just follows the road to the top. When the snow is good, the Brian Head ski area operates a snowcat that allows alpine skiers to ski the steep chutes off the top. The resort wants to build a lift that would bring skiers to a spot just below the peak's ridge.

Murphy says avalanche danger is usually quite low, but severe weather can sometimes cause whiteouts in the flat meadow east of the peak. Skiers should check at Brian Head Nordic or with the ski area about weather conditions before making a winter ascent.

Jacklin said volunteers from the Sierra Club helped to restore the CCC-built viewing structure at the top of the mountain. The patio was repaired, the old wooden beams repainted, and a new trail built leading from the parking area. More interpretive signs will be put into the area in the future.

Geologically, Brian Head Peak consists of rhyolite, an acidic material that consists of welded tuff and ash. Volcanic activity 38 million years ago also left basalt flows lapping into the side of the mountain. And, there are signs of glaciers.

— *Tom Wharton*

Summit:	12,087 ft.
Difficulty:	Moderate to difficult.
USGS maps:	Indian Farm Creek, Ibapah Peak.
Length:	6.25 miles from first car park; 5 miles from second car park.

Trailhead: In Callao, a road runs north-south on the east side of the Deep Creeks. From Callao turn south on this road. Watch for a road labeled Granite Creek, where you turn right. About 4.5 miles up the road is a stream crossing that most vehicles cannot make. Park here and walk the road for about 1.25 miles. This road ends in a clearing, with a faint trail leading right toward the stream. Follow this across the brook, then onto a sagebrush slope where the trail splits. Follow the fork to the left, which makes a sharp turn. This trail crosses a subsidiary ridge and goes up a valley. The trail is faint, so keep in mind that you want to reach the ridge at the top of this drainage. Once on the ridge, Ibapah Peak is to the north. Hike on the east side, just off the ridge top and you will soon find a trail. This is a good path that switchbacks to the top of Ibapah. You will know Ibapah Peak by the wooden and rock structures on top. Part of this was a heliograph station dating from the 1880s.

The hike: If a contest were held to determine the Utah mountain range with the wackiest and most fascinating lore, the Deep Creeks on the Utah-Nevada border would win. Judge for yourself.

— Orrin Porter Rockwell, bodyguard for early Mormon President Brigham Young, and a band of church members found six Indian bodies standing bolt upright and crusted over with salt deposits in springs on the Deep Creeks' foothills.

— Albert Ross Goddin built a rock cabin with gunports in a Deep Creek canyon to hide from Jesse James. Goddin, allegedly the stable boy for James, squealed on the outlaw, landing the latter in jail. Goddin lived the rest of his life in the mountain hideaway.

— Then there is the wandering-elk tale. In the late 1980s, Nevada game wardens wanted elk in the state. They purchased some from Utah. A few were given to the Goshute Indians on the Nevada side of the Deep Creeks. The elk didn't like the area. They picked up and moved home to Utah. Now there is a healthy elk herd on the Utah side of the Deep Creeks.

If amusing stories aren't enough, the Deep Creeks are a wilderness study area with Juab County's highest peak. Ibapah Peak is 12,087 feet. The name is a Goshute word meaning "white clay water" for the fine particles in the streams.

This is a mountain range that began gathering human history with Ameri-

JUAB COUNTY — IBAPAH PEAK

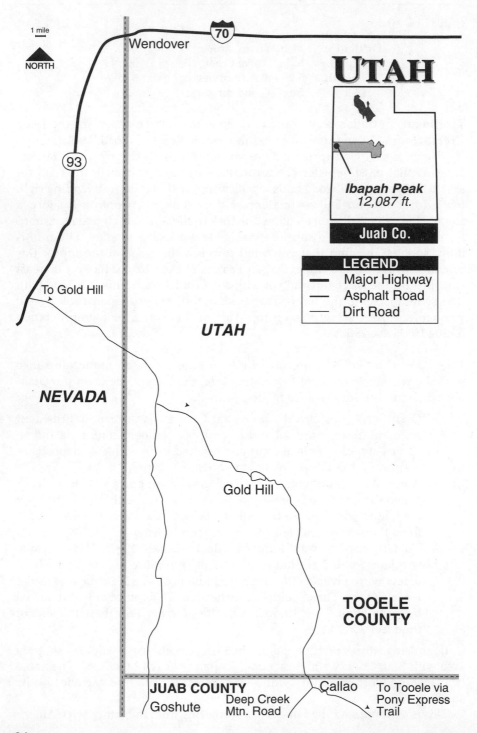

1 mile

NORTH

Wendover

70

93

UTAH

Ibapah Peak
12,087 ft.

Juab Co.

LEGEND
Major Highway
Asphalt Road
Dirt Road

To Gold Hill

UTAH

NEVADA

Gold Hill

TOOELE COUNTY

JUAB COUNTY

Goshute

Deep Creek
Mtn. Road

Callao

To Tooele via
Pony Express
Trail

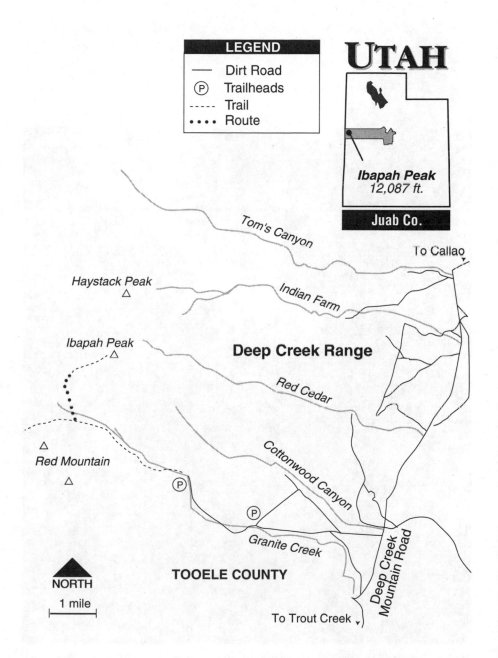

LEGEND
— Dirt Road
Ⓟ Trailheads
----- Trail
•••• Route

UTAH

Ibapah Peak
12,087 ft.

Juab Co.

Tom's Canyon

To Callao

Haystack Peak
△

Indian Farm

Ibapah Peak
△

Deep Creek Range

Red Cedar

△

Red Mountain

△

Ⓟ

Cottonwood Canyon

Ⓟ

Granite Creek

Deep Creek Mountain Road

NORTH

1 mile

TOOELE COUNTY

To Trout Creek

Red Mountain is on the same ridgeline leading to Ibapah, Juab County's highest peak. Paula Huff

can Indians. Fremonts inhabited the Deep Creeks—in the heart of the Great Basin—followed by the Goshute. They left their mark: petroglyphs and pictographs at some canyon mouths.

The origin of the Fremont and Goshute is sketchy, but they were "flexible and adaptable" people, said David Madsen, state paleoecologist. The harsh environment made it impossible for them to live in large groups, so they wandered in bands of 25 of 30 people. Where farming was good, corn, beans, and squash were grown. Wild animals, seeds, and plants were collected, too. They were hunters and gatherers in places where it was too hot for farming.

The Deep Creeks' mountain sheep, deer, and antelope were certainly part of the native diet. But crickets and rodents were more plentiful and took less effort to catch.

In 1859, Great Basin explorer J.H. Simpson watched a successful Goshute hunter untie several rats from a string around his waist, according to Ronald Bateman, author of *Deep Creek Reflections: 125 Years of Settlement at Ibapah, Utah*. A cook scorched the rodents in a fire, then rubbed off the hair. Feces were squeezed out, and the entrails removed with a finger. In a kettle hung from a three-legged tripod, soup was made with the meat and bones.

As for crickets, they were a delicacy. After being driven into furrows and lighted on fire, they were pounded into flour and mixed with berries. "Desert fruitcake" is what Madsen calls these biscuits.

A bigger score were piles of locust that had dropped into Great Salt Lake and washed onto shore. Salted and naturally preserved, the insects were easily scooped into baskets for food. They taste like beer nuts, Madsen claims.

Two years after the Mormons arrived in the Salt Lake Valley, the Goshute lifestyle in the Deep Creeks was disrupted. The Indians were accustomed to locating their camps near streams and canyon mouths to take advantage of water and available food. Now whites were making permanent settlements, sawmills, and gristmills there.

"Virtually all of Utah's towns sit on archaeological sites," said Madsen. "Where water comes down from the canyons and goes out onto an alluvial fan, that's where the Indians farmed. So did the pioneers."

By 1859, cattle, sheep, and horses grazed much of the Goshutes' ranges. Hostilities—usually motivated by lack of food—resulted in the federal government trying to teach the Goshutes to farm near present-day Ibapah. That failed. Attempts to relocate them to the Ute reservation in the Uinta Basin fell short, too. Finally on March 23, 1914, President William Howard Taft created the Goshute Indian Reservation. These days, 109 Indians live on the reservation.

Goshute Genevieve Fields still hikes through the Deep Creeks collecting wild carrots, potatoes and onions. She also gathers pine nuts. Tobacco grows there, too.

"My parents and grandparents would dry these plants. It was their winter food. I freeze them," said Fields, who has lived her entire life on the reservation. "I don't think the younger people do this anymore. But the older people do. I take my grandson up when I go picking, because if I don't show him, he will never know."

A Pony Express station was built at present-day Callao in 1860. After 1 1/2 years, the telegraph ran the horse-based mail system into the ground. The E. W. Tripp family purchased the station for a ranch. Others soon followed with their sheep.

Cecil Bates remembers herding sheep up Granite Canyon, over Ibapah Peak and down Red Cedar Canyon. A packhorse once spooked near the peak and began bucking as it ran downhill. Camp supplies were thrown willy-nilly, including the precious sourdough starter, their source of daily bread.

"My brother and I would find a little gob of sourdough on a rock and we would gather it up," said 80-year-old Bates. "We gathered enough to keep the sourdough going, and it was just as good as it had been before."

Fishing with a piece of string tied to a birch tree limb was another of Bates' favorite pastimes. The rare Bonneville cutthroat was often the catch.

The Deep Creeks and other isolated mountains are called "island ecosystems." Bristlecone pines dating back 2,000 years are found on high ridges. Wildlife is trapped in these oases by miles of flat, salty, waterless desert surrounding the peaks.

Bonneville cutthroat are an example. When ancient Lake Bonneville dried up, these fish made their home in the Deep Creeks, Bear River, and Bear Lake, says Mark Pierce, biologist for the Bureau of Land Management office in Fillmore. Bonneville cutthroat have scattered, round spots on the upper portion of their silver-gray to charcoal-colored bodies. Subtle hues of pink are on their flanks during spawning. The Deep Creeks are open to general fishing.

Isolation created a healthy population of cougar, too. Forty bighorn sheep were introduced in the Deep Creeks in the 1980s. All were killed by mountain lions. One biologist picked up the collar of a dead sheep and was followed back to his car by a cougar.

Cattle and sheep now graze in the Deep Creeks, regardless of the cougar. And there are nine working mines getting flagstone, magnesite, tungsten, gold and silver from the mountain.

The Spanish may have mined the Deep Creeks as early as 1805, says Bateman. And there are written records saying Indians offered ore samples to travelers in exchange for tobacco. But it was the gold seekers bound for California who began seriously digging the precious metal in the Deep Creeks.

By 1917 there was enough mining to warrant a railroad spur to the Gold Hill area. The last trip of the Deep Creek Railroad was July 28, 1939. The site boomed again in World War II when arsenic was needed. Now it is a ghost town with a pure-breed horse raiser and summer homes, Bateman said.

"When I was a kid, the whole community [of Ibapah] would go to the Queen of Sheba gold mine," he recalls. "We would ride in the back of a cattle truck. We would spend the day fishing and having a picnic."

— *Paula Huff*

13 KANE COUNTY — UNNAMED PEAK (PROPOSED NAME—ANDY NELSON PEAK)

Summit:	10,027 ft.
Difficulty:	Easy.
USGS map:	Navajo Lake.
Length:	1.75 miles.

Trailhead: From Cedar City, drive east on State Road 14 up Cedar Canyon. Take the Navajo Lake turnoff, about 26 miles from Cedar City. Park about 0.1 mile past the Te-ah Campground, the last on the southwest side of the lake. The section of Virgin River Rim Trail going toward Kane County's highest peak is on the left or south side of the road. Begin walking this hard-

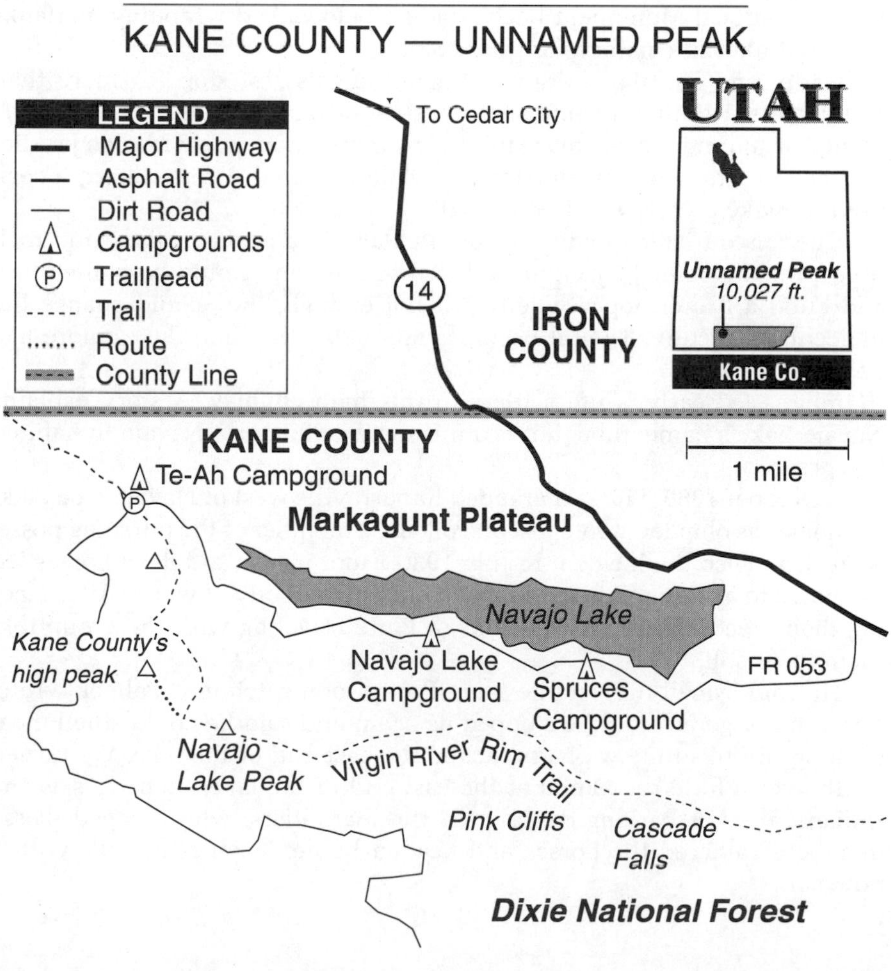

KANE COUNTY — UNNAMED PEAK

LEGEND
— Major Highway
— Asphalt Road
— Dirt Road
△ Campgrounds
Ⓟ Trailhead
---- Trail
······ Route
==== County Line

To Cedar City

UTAH

Unnamed Peak
10,027 ft.

Kane Co.

IRON
COUNTY

14

KANE COUNTY
△ Te-Ah Campground

Markagunt Plateau

1 mile

Navajo Lake

Kane County's
high peak △

Navajo Lake
Campground

Spruces
Campground

FR 053

Navajo
Lake Peak

Virgin River Rim Trail

Pink Cliffs

Cascade
Falls

Dixie National Forest

packed hiking/mountain biking/equestrian trail. In about two miles, pass the junction with the Lodge Trail, continuing on the Virgin River Rim Trail. In about 0.5 mile, the trail reaches a saddle between two peaks. The peak to the right is Kane County's highest. There is no trail, but it is easy walking to the top.

Kane County is one of two counties in Utah that has a point higher than the tallest peak. A ridgeline leading to Gooseberry Point on the northwest side of Navajo Lake reaches 10,080 feet before exiting the county.

The hike: "Terrible and beautiful wasteland.... Colored by every color of the spectrum.... Sculpted by sandblast winds.... Carved, broken and split by canyons so deep and narrow that the rivers run in sunless depths."

That's how author Wallace Stegner described Kane County in his 1942 book *Mormon Country*. It also could be a word picture of the view from Kane County's highest peak, an unnamed point at 10,027 feet. Rising from the shore of Navajo Lake, this gently sloping mound has the Virgin River's headwater bubbling from its south face. The colorfully warped landscape of Cedar Breaks National Monument begins fading below. And wrapping its flanks are the Pink Cliffs, named for their color.

Beauty and food have drawn humans to this rest stop for more than 8,000 years. Hunting, fishing and a variety of plants led the Anasazi, Fremont, Navajo and Piute to make this their summer home, said Marian Jacklin, heritage program coordinator for the Dixie National Forest. Chert, a rock used to make points, was another pull.

"Chert is difficult to chip; it doesn't flake like obsidian [volcanic rock used to make points]," Jacklin said. "So the Indians would bury the chert and build a fire on top. By getting it hot enough, they could change the molecular structure. Then it becomes more glasslike, and flakes more like obsidian."

Indians led early white settlers to this high country. A story explains Navajo Lake's name, though it is a misnomer. Piute, not Navajo, inhabited this area.

In October 1869, Piutes marauded Kanarraville west of Navajo Lake, taking horses as plunder, wrote Joseph Pollock, a member of the pursuing posse, who chronicled the incident in July 1930. Hoof marks and dead horses led the posse to a mountain overlooking an unknown body of water. After leading their steeds down a steep slope, a Piute traveling with the group told them to be still.

"He could smell fire, and he said, 'Pretty soon catchum," Pollock wrote. "We did not go far until he stopped us again and said he could smell meat cooking. By this time we had reached the east end of the lake. We turned south over a little rock knoll at the east end of the lake, then we saw the Indians' fire." A barking dog alerted the marauders, who escaped. Posse members gathered the horses and headed home, leaving the lake with a new name.

The trail near Kane County's highest peak offers views of red rock country like the Pink Cliffs and Zion National Park. Paula Huff

Known as *Pa-ca-ay*—Cloud Lake—to the Piute, this basin of water and the mountains around it are the result of volcanic activity that formed the Markagunt Plateau, where Kane County's high peak rises. Locals call it Cedar Mountain.

First beach-front property, then part of a mountainous area draining into an inland sea stretching from the Gulf of Mexico to the Arctic Ocean, this landscape saw "violent volcanic activity" about 30 million years ago, said Andy Godfrey, geomorphologist for the USDA Forest Service regional office in Ogden.

Geologic forces that created the Basin and Range then heaved the earth upward, more than a mile above its former level. Lava oozed from fissures and spatter cones after that. Some of this ooze plugged the natural drainage of Navajo Lake, leaving the water to worm its way downward into tunnels that now create Cascade Falls, south of the lake.

This lake still drains through these lava tubes. Levels fluctuated dramatically—sometimes leaving it dry mid-summer—until the Civilian Conservation Corps built a dike. As a result, Nephi Jones' ranch lost water in 1942, said Alva Matheson.

"His water came out of the lake and worked its way south through the hills," said Matheson, a Cedar City author and historian. "When they put the dam in, it shut off the water, so he went and dynamited the dam. That caused a stir." After a court battle, Jones paid $2,000. The dam was moved higher, and Jones' water restored.

Though Navajo Lake's water rises and falls yearly, it remains a favorite fishing spot. Division of Wildlife Resources officials plant rainbow and brown trout. Three campgrounds and two lodges provide a resting spot for summer anglers.

Volunteers and the USDA Forest Service finished a hiking, Mountain biking, and equestrian trail near Navajo Lake three years ago. This route to Kane County's high peak is loaded with spectacular scenery. Bristlecone pines, some of the oldest living trees on Earth, dot the high points.

"Around this area, the pines are 1,500 to 2,000 years old," said Mike Martin of the USDA Forest Service Cedar City Ranger District. "In some parts of Nevada they are up to 4,000 years old."

In 1918, Lee Bower and some of Matheson's other chums grew tired of school and drove their Star car to Navajo Lake for a day of fishing.

"They just got the boat on the lake and got out part way when here comes their car rolling down into the lake," the 93-year-old Matheson said. "They were so anxious to get back to their car that they tipped over and nearly drowned. When they finally got to the car a man passed by with a wagon. They talked him into putting the horses onto the car and pulling it back onto the road."

— *Paula Huff*

14 MILLARD COUNTY — MINE CAMP PEAK

Summit:	10,222 ft.
Difficulty:	Moderate.
USGS maps:	Mt. Catherine, White Pine Peak, Sunset Peak.
Length:	5.75 miles.

Trailhead: From Fillmore, head east on 200 South Canyon Road. This street is the start of the Chalk Creek Road. Drive to the Pistol Rock Picnic Site. About 0.2 mile past this area, a spur goes to the right, while the main road heads left. The spur is labeled "Bear Canyon-Pine Creek Trail." This is the trailhead. Follow the trail, which crosses a wide creek many times, to the Bear Canyon Trail intersection. Take Bear Canyon Trail, then begin following signs to Paradise Canyon. Once in Paradise Canyon, the trail becomes faint. Walk through the canyon, and climb to the ridge at its headwall. Mine Camp Peak will be to the north. This is a pleasant walk until the ridge climb begins. From the ridge, it is an easy—though steep—walk to Mine Camp Peak.

The hike: Hikers making their way to the top of 10,222-foot Mine Camp Peak located east of Utah's territorial capital will quickly notice three things: Water, old sawmill equipment, and mines.

That is appropriate. Millard County's tallest peak is located in the midst of flowing water and evidence of sawmill activity. Signs of lumber, mining, and rusting equipment can be seen along much of the upper portion of the 6-mile trail.

Mine Camp Peak is located in the Pahvant Range of central Utah. In the language of the Native Americans, Pahvant means "close to water," "down to water," or "by the water." Hikers soon discover why. From the start of the trail where man-made fish structures help trout production on Chalk Creek, to spots near the top of the mountain, water seems to flow everywhere.

During the spring and much of the summer when winter snowfall is heavy, waterfalls from side canyons dump into the main stream. Hikers walk through high country swamps filled with quaking aspens and skunk cabbage. Wildflowers, like arrowleaf balsamroot and mountain bluebell, decorate the trail.

According to Linda Jackson of the Fishlake National Forest, Mine Camp Peak is composed of ocean sediments that were deposited approximately 500 million years ago in an ocean with characteristics similar to the present south Atlantic Ocean.

"At the time of deposition," she said, "this part of Utah was a seashore on the western edge of the North American continent. Over millions of years, the continent drifted eastward toward the European continent, and finally westward again. Mine Camp Peak obtained its present elevation due to the eventual expansion of the continent which formed the wide basins and nar-

MILLARD COUNTY — MINE CAMP PEAK

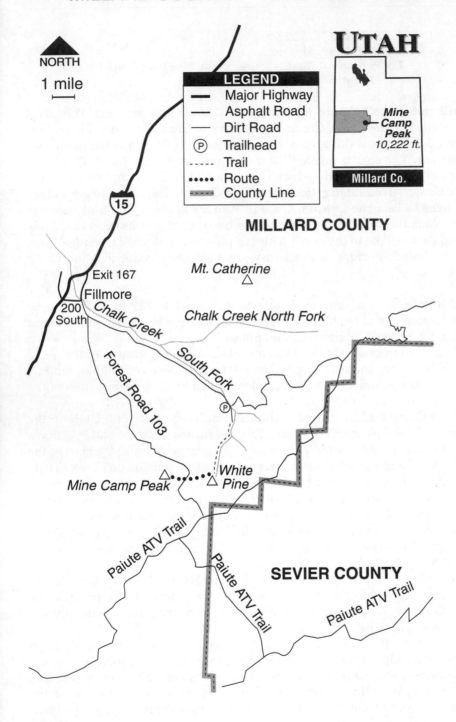

NORTH

1 mile

LEGEND
▬▬▬	Major Highway
▬▬	Asphalt Road
───	Dirt Road
Ⓟ	Trailhead
- - - -	Trail
••••	Route
▓▓▓	County Line

UTAH

Mine Camp Peak
10,222 ft.

Millard Co.

MILLARD COUNTY

15

Exit 167

Mt. Catherine

Fillmore

200 South

Chalk Creek

Chalk Creek North Fork

South Fork

Forest Road 103

Ⓟ

Mine Camp Peak

White Pine

Paiute ATV Trail

Paiute ATV Trail

SEVIER COUNTY

Paiute ATV Trail

At the right time of year, wildflowers like arrowleaf balsamroot and lupine are thick in canyons leading to Mine Camp Peak, Millard County's highest peak.
Paula Huff

row ranges that we see today."

Those driving on US 89 through Sevier County looking at the east-facing slopes of the Pahvant Range might notice streaks of red rock at the base of the mountains. Salt Lake geologist Genevieve Atwood says that is because some of those deposits were laid down by predecessors of the Sevier River formation which filled in the flanks of the Sevier Valley.

"When you see red," she said, "you are often looking at sedimentary rocks that were laid down by water, but not in a water body. It was laid down in a mud flat or a stream bed and exposed to air. As a result, you end up with red-looking rocks. Red is rust. You may have bits of iron-colored rock. By the time the iron has been laid down again in those sediments, it is turned to rust. This is an area with interesting mineralogy associated with igneous activity."

The abundance of these minerals resulted in some commercial mining in the area. According to Jackson, the Osceola gold mine was located at the head of Pine Creek, less than one mile northeast of what is now known as Mine Camp Peak. Utah Historical Society records show that gypsum, sulphur, pyrite and fluorite mines were also located in the area.

Still, the origin of the name "Mine Camp Peak" remains somewhat obscure. The forest service, Utah Historical Society, and local historians aren't certain who named the peak or which mine camp gave it its name. The evidence of mine pits near the top of the trail would indicate that the peak was named to honor an old mining camp in the area.

Many Millard County residents think that nearby Mt. Catherine, named after an early surveyor's wife, is the tallest peak in the county. Writers and historians who worked on the 1939 Work Project Administration Utah guide made that mistake. They listed the 10,020-foot Mt. Catherine as the tallest in the county.

Miners and people building pioneer towns also harvested timber off the Pahvants. According to long-time Millard County resident Brent Olson, a conservation officer with the Division of Wildlife Resources, hikers can see a wide variety of wildlife when scaling the summit of Mine Camp Peak.

"The area has mule deer and an expanding elk herd," said Olson. "We have one of the best mountain lion units in the state. There is an occasional sighting of a bear. There are coyote, forest grouse and an expanding population of Rio Grande turkeys."

From Mine Camp Peak—marked by a rock cairn—hikers can look west across the basins and ranges of the Great Basin. On a clear day, they can see the Deep Creeks and Nevada's Great Basin National Park and Mt. Moriah. To the east, the road cut for Interstate 70 is easily seen, along with a section of the Fishlake National Forest. And, of course, there is evidence of the mines and the flowing water that give the area its name.

— *Paula Huff and Tom Wharton*

15 RICH COUNTY — UNNAMED PEAK (PROPOSED NAME—BRIDGER PEAK)

Summit:	9,255.
Difficulty:	Easy.
USGS map:	Garden City.
Length:	1 mile.

Trailhead: From 400 North in Logan, drive east on Highway 89. This is the Logan Canyon road. Drive about 20 miles. Begin looking for the Utah Department of Transportation highway maintenance buildings on the left side of the road. About 0.5 mile past these buildings turn left onto the road marked Swan Flat. Drive about 2.75 miles on this road until reaching Swan Flat, a lush, swampy meadow. As you enter Swan Flat, notice the blocked-off dirt road to the right. Park and hike along this steep road, which ascends a ridge. When the road takes a sharp right, leave it, and begin bushwacking in a northeasterly direction. This peak is difficult to find because the terrain is rolling and covered with trees. The 7.5 Garden City quad will help. There is a small cairn marking the peak.

The hike: Near the foot of Rich County's highest peak, Thomas "Pegleg" Smith once spun tales for road-weary immigrants who bought vegetables and grains from his trading post. Losing his leg was a favorite yarn for this

A hiker plays on the ridgeline leading to Rich County's highest peak. In the background is Mt. Naomi, Cache County's highest peak. Paula Huff

former trapper, who operated an outpost from 1843 to 1850. Either an Indian bullet shattered the foot and calf or an arrow poisoned it during a fall hunting trip, depending on the version. No foreigner to embellishment, Pegleg sometimes claimed he amputated it himself. Other times, he said partner James Cockrell helped.

Whatever happened, Pegleg ended up being Bear Lake's most famous mountain man, according to Robert E. Parson, author of *A History of Rich County*. In this northeast county of Utah his reputation stands with many characters who roamed the vales and hills.

At 9,255 feet, Rich County's highest peak is nameless. A *Salt Lake Tribune* contest has proposed the moniker Bridger Peak, commemorating mountain man Jim Bridger, who sought beaver in nearby creeks.

Bear Lake's emerald-green waters lie to the east of the high point. Bear River Range's Naomi and Doubletop peaks create a jutting horizon to the west. With squinted eyes the Bear River can be seen to the north. Highway of the overland traveler, its meanders map the Oregon Trail.

Long before trappers and settlers ground a westward route into this soil, Rich County's rocks show it was a shallow marine environment located much closer to the equator, said Sue Morgan, lecturer in Utah State University's geology department.

Over millions of years the water level dropped. The land shifted eastward. The earth stretched apart. Valleys and mountains formed. Rich County's high point was among these ranges, heaving to the sky sedimentary rock pocked with marine fossils. In the midst of all this, a musk ox and baby columbian mammoth died near Bear Lake about 11,000 years ago. Their jaw bones and teeth are in David Gillete's hands.

"Finding their bones was not a surprise, but it adds a couple more small pieces to the puzzle of how life was before us," said Gillette, Utah State paleontologist.

Musk ox are related to cows and bison. In modern times they live high in the Arctic. But these animals—more compact than a buffalo and with backwards curling horns—once wandered as far south as the Gulf Coast. Some thought this meant the Gulf Coast was a cold climate, said Gillette. Actually, the extinct cousin of the musk ox living in the south was more heat tolerant. Columbian mammoths, an extinct relative of modern elephants, lived with the musk ox near a freshwater lake fed by high-mountain glaciers. The climate was much cooler than today.

Little is known about the prehistoric tribes who moved through Rich County when mammoths and musk ox rambled. Archaeologists have hardly set spade to dirt in this country, said David Madsen, Utah State paleoecologist. Written records tell of summer festivals when Chief Bear Hunter's Northwest Shoshoni and Chief Washakie's Eastern Shoshoni gathered on the southwest shore of Bear Lake, said Brigham Madsen, author of *The Shoshoni Frontier and the Bear River Massacre*.

"It was a real fair; they gambled, raced horses, did a little courting and had big feasts, just like our own barbecues," said Madsen, University of Utah professor emeritus of history.

RICH COUNTY — UNNAMED PEAK

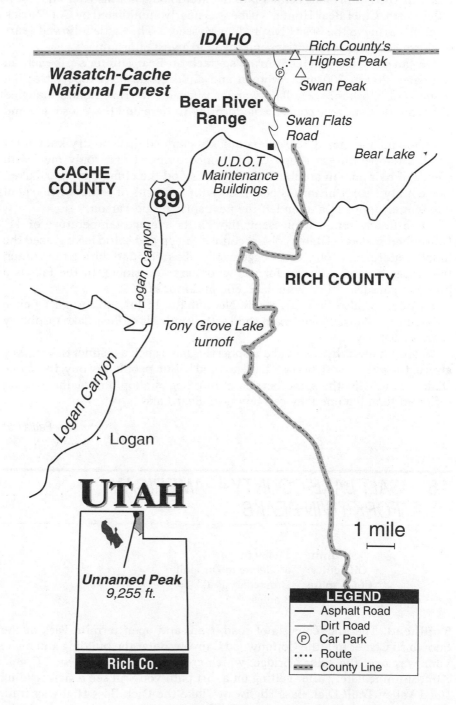

IDAHO

Rich County's
Highest Peak

Wasatch-Cache
National Forest

Swan Peak

Bear River
Range

Swan Flats
Road

Bear Lake

CACHE
COUNTY

U.D.O.T
Maintenance
Buildings

89

RICH COUNTY

Logan Canyon

Tony Grove Lake
turnoff

Logan Canyon

Logan

UTAH

1 mile

Unnamed Peak
9,255 ft.

Rich Co.

LEGEND
— Asphalt Road
— Dirt Road
Ⓟ Car Park
.... Route
==== County Line

Mountain men rendezvoused on Bear Lake's south shore in 1827 and 1828. In 1863, Mormons settled into the area. Four months later and a few miles north, Chief Bear Hunter's tribe was nearly annihilated by Col. Patrick Connor's army in the Bear River Indian Massacre. The battle followed years of skirmishes between settlers and the Northwest Shoshoni.

On Jan. 29, 1863, the U.S. Army's attack on Bear Hunter's tribe left an estimated 200 to 300 men, women and children dead. A reporter at the scene said Shoshoni were left "warrior piled on warrior, horses mangled and wounded in every conceivable form, with here and there a squaw and papoose."

Following the massacre, settlers quickly claimed this country known for its cold temperatures. Joseph C. Rich once quipped that "only men with plenty of hair on 'em are tough enough to stand the climate of Bear Lake." The county's early history is peppered with accounts of settlers who spent one winter in the area, then left the next spring, said Parson.

Some finally found it pleasant, though its average temperature of 41° Fahrenheit makes it Utah's coldest county. Sheep and cattle have grazed the hills for more than 100 years. Loggers still take trees, and during the winter, the slopes become a haven for snowmobilers and skiers. In the fall its a hunter's paradise, filled with deer, elk, and moose.

Raspberries also find this a suitable climate. In July and August Renee LaBeau's Garden City ice cream shop sells hundreds of Bear Lake raspberry shakes each day.

"I don't know why Bear Lake raspberries have such a distinct flavor; they are just a sweet, soft berry," LaBeau said. "But people do buy the same shake made with the same berries at our Logan shop and claim it tastes different than the one they can buy near Bear Lake."

— Paula Huff

16 SALT LAKE COUNTY — AMERICAN FORK TWIN PEAKS

Summit:	11,489 ft.
Difficulty:	Moderate to Difficult.
USGS map:	Dromedary Peak.
Length:	3 miles.

Trailhead: The hike consists of road, trail, and open terrain. Park at the Snowbird Center in Little Cottonwood Canyon. Enter the building and make your way over the skier's bridge, which crosses Little Cottonwood Creek. Almost immediately after getting on a dirt path you will see a sign reading "Gad Valley Trail/ Dick Bass Highway." Take the Dick Bass Highway trail. After 15 minutes you will reach a T. Turn left. Walk until you reach the

SALT LAKE COUNTY — AMERICAN FORK TWIN PEAKS

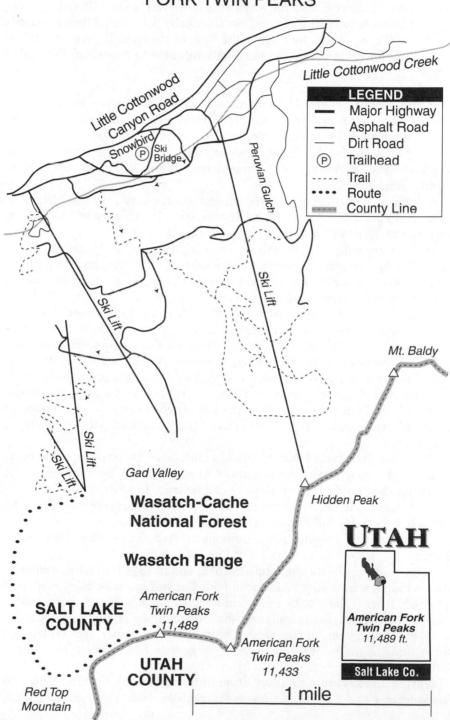

Little Cottonwood Creek

Little Cottonwood Canyon Road

Snowbird
Ⓟ Ski Bridge

Peruvian Gulch

LEGEND
- ▬ Major Highway
- — Asphalt Road
- — Dirt Road
- Ⓟ Trailhead
- ---- Trail
- •••• Route
- ░░░ County Line

Ski Lift

Ski Lift

Mt. Baldy △

Ski Lift

Ski Lift

Gad Valley

Wasatch-Cache National Forest

Wasatch Range

△ Hidden Peak

UTAH

SALT LAKE COUNTY

American Fork Twin Peaks
△ *11,489*

△ American Fork Twin Peaks *11,433*

UTAH COUNTY

Red Top Mountain

American Fork Twin Peaks 11,489 ft.

Salt Lake Co.

1 mile

Wilbere chairlift, where there is another T. Turn right onto a trail labeled "Gad Valley." The trail comes to a Y in about 15 minutes. Take the right fork. After crossing a brook, take the trail to the left. From here walk to the top of the Gad Valley II chairlift. Ski runs from this chairlift are called Bass-ackwards and Little Cloud. Climb the ridge to the right of the chairlift, which is talus-covered. Follow this rocky, but easy-walking ridge to American Fork Twin Peaks.

The hike: Mining Miller Hill in American Fork Canyon was becoming expensive and discouraging for George Tyng. He resolved to stop pouring money into holes. The lease would expire in a few months anyway, at the end of 1904. But while installing new mine-car track, Tyng's miners struck silver and lead. The sparkling metals poured into chutes like sand. He was instantly rich.

By chipping into this ore, Tyng also made his way into the history of American Fork Twin Peaks, the highest in Salt Lake County at 11,489 feet. Unfortunately, he did not live to enjoy the wealth.

Tyng's story links into the history of mining in the central Wasatch Mountains. Easterners were becoming suspicious of the Mormons. Reports of polygamy and other strange practices were circulating. East coasters began contemplating strategies. Mining was the solution.

Colonel Patrick Connor's tactic was to take an Army detachment into the Utah territory, find valuable minerals, attract gentiles and dilute Mormon Church influence. By 1863, he was marching his California soldiers past the governor's mansion as a band played to announce their arrival. Within one year, Connor's men had discovered silver, lead, and gold in the hills.

These precious metals were found in American Fork Canyon, too, on the south side of Twin Peaks. But as in the Cottonwood canyons, mining didn't begin in earnest until 1870, when narrow-gauge railroads were built in the canyons.

American Fork Twin Peaks hikers can still see aerial tramways that cross ridges and swoop down the canyon. Old roads—built by engineers who thumbed their noses at steep slopes—can be traced to heaps of orange tailings on every side of the summits. And it's easy to imagine mules pulling green animal hides full of ore across snow in the winter.

Though mining attracted non-Mormons to Utah, the livelihood was short-lived.

"The mines gave out completely in 1876, and in 1878 the railroad closed," Alexis Kelner writes about American Fork Canyon in the original edition of *Wasatch Tours*. "The tracks were removed for salvage, so all that remains today...is a roadbed, many trails and abandoned mines, and scores of names."

Silver Bell, Queen of the West, Orphan, Silver Dipper and Whirlwind were some of the mines' names. And, of course, there was Tyng's Miller Hill.

During a second mining surge around the turn of the century, Tyng and his youngest son, Francis, began working Miller Hill. The year was 1902.

The mine sits on a ridge leading to Twin Peaks. The duo's first winter was spent in a cabin near a tunnel at 10,000 feet. Two years passed until they found precious metals.

"They offered five dollars per ton for hauling ore to American Fork," according to a 1969 article by Laurence P. James in *Journal of the West*. "Twenty teams of horses worked steadily but more were needed. Tons of ore were stored in cloth sacks on Dutchman Flat, after being dragged down from the mine over the snow."

The next winter brought heavy snowfall. On Jan. 19, Tyng was keeping books in a lean-to away from the mining camp when an avalanche crushed the building. Tyng was found with a pencil still in hand. A nail from a falling roof beam had penetrated his skull.

A crude sleigh was made to carry the body to American Fork. One miner recalled the trip as the most nerve-wracking of his life. But after hauling Tyng to the village below, they decided to lay him to rest near Miller Hill, as his will said. The site was at a view he often admired. His body was carried back up the peak, and 11 days later he was buried 0.25 mile east of the mine.

It is easy to understand Tyng's choice for his grave. There is little vegetation near Twin Peaks, affording vistas of Timpanogos, Box Elder Peak, the jagged ridge line separating Little Cottonwood Canyon from American Fork Canyon, and the Uintas on a clear day. The Great Salt Lake is a moody blue. Since the 1920s, hikers also have been able to spot mountain goats.

A hiker climbs the ridgeline to American Fork Twin Peaks, Salt Lake County's highest peak, with the Salt Lake Valley in the background. Paula Huff

Fifteen years after Tyng's death, mining was almost nonexistent in the central Wasatch. Sawmills—providing lumber for Salt Lakers and the mines—were defunct because the trees were gone. Cattle and sheep had grazed hillsides until they were denuded. Slopes in American Fork Canyon were terraced to prevent further erosion. Animals were locked out of Big Cottonwood and Little Cottonwood to protect city dwellers' water.

"The [central Wasatch] Mountains were just sitting quietly in the '30s, '40s and '50s," said Charles Keller, a historian and longtime Wasatch hiker. "Then skiing started and things got built up again."

For American Fork Twin Peaks skiing means Snowbird, a resort in Little Cottonwood Canyon that sits on USDA Forest Service property. It opened in January 1972. Snowbird's aerial tram stops on a ridge that leads to the most easterly Twin Peak. Skiers often parallel this jackknife edge and move into a large bowl known for avalanches.

"One of the most active slide paths in the area comes off Twin Peaks," said Rick May, Snowbird's creative production manager. "It is called 'Old Reliable' because it slides every time someone shoots it."

For Bob Bonar, Twin Peaks means "the pipeline." He calls it a "classic ski adventure," and only the courageous—or crazy—ski the pipeline, said Bonar, a Snowbird employee since the resort opened.

Skiers ride the tram to Hidden Peak, ski down toward the base of Twin Peaks, then take their skis off to walk back up. There is a little rock climbing involved, too. At the pipeline's brink, skiers lower themselves down into the shoot, which is close to vertical.

— *Paula Huff*

17 *SEVIER COUNTY — FISH LAKE HIGHTOP*

Summit:	11,633 ft.
Difficulty:	Moderate.
USGS map:	Fish Lake
Length:	5.5 miles.

Trailhead: From Highway 24 turn onto Highway 25, the Fish Lake road. Drive to the Pelican Point trailhead. The well-defined trail heads across a sagebrush flat and drops into Pelican Canyon. It climbs to a saddle, then ascends the hightop. From there it is an undulating ski or walk through a pine forest.

When taking a hike, consider bringing a sack to carry out garbage. Not only should you pick up your own garbage, but try to leave the area cleaner than you found it by picking up the trash left by others.

The hike: Some want to swim the English Channel. Some set records by stroking around Manhattan Island. Carvel Mattsson's friend Marius Salisbury

SEVIER COUNTY — FISH LAKE HIGHTOP

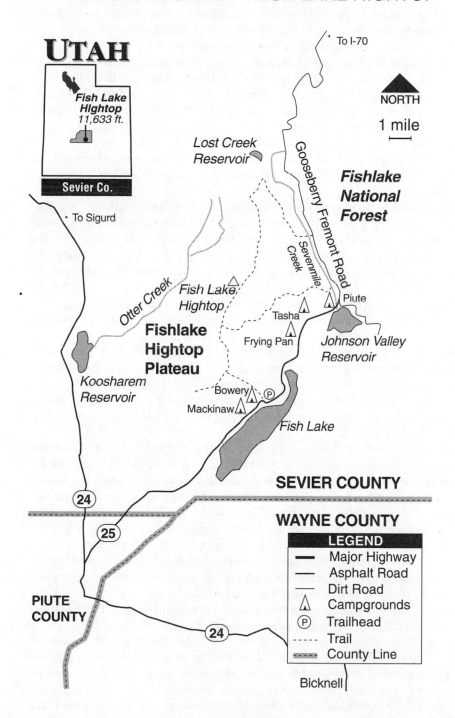

UTAH

Fish Lake Hightop
11,633 ft.

Sevier Co.

To I-70

NORTH

1 mile

Lost Creek Reservoir

Fishlake National Forest

To Sigurd

Gooseberry Fremont Road

Sevenmile Creek

Piute

Fish Lake Hightop

Tasha

Fishlake Hightop Plateau

Frying Pan

Johnson Valley Reservoir

Otter Creek

Koosharem Reservoir

Bowery

Mackinaw

Fish Lake

SEVIER COUNTY

24

WAYNE COUNTY

25

LEGEND	
▬▬	Major Highway
—	Asphalt Road
⊥	Dirt Road
△	Campgrounds
Ⓟ	Trailhead
- - -	Trail
▓▓▓	County Line

PIUTE COUNTY

24

Bicknell

wanted to swim the deep, frigid Fish Lake in central Utah, a body of water sitting at the base of Fish Lake Hightop, the highest peak in Sevier County. When the friends conceived the idea in 1931, Fish Lake's cold water had a reputation for making people hypothermic and killing them. So, to the 23-year-old Richfield residents, this was an adventure.

"We got the biggest can of wagon grease at a blacksmith shop, and I absolutely covered him with it," said Mattson, who got the idea from articles about English Channel swimmers. "The grease turned him brown-ish-green. It was a sight to behold." A rope tied around Salisbury's ankle was held by Mattson as he rowed behind. Then Salisbury took the plunge, swimming 1.5 miles across the widest section of lake.

"For all the planning, it was an uneventful swim," said Mattsson, an 88-year-old retired Salt Lake City attorney, whose life-long friend has since died.

Fish Lake Hightop gets its name from the excellent fishing, in a lake 120-feet deep in places. It is an area that has attracted humans—and their antics—for centuries. Fremont Indians built summer homes on the lake's shore nearly 1,000 years ago, according to Joel Janetski, Brigham Young University archaeologist and associate professor of anthropology. Others gathered roots and bulbs about 300 years after the birth of Christ.

"The native peoples were up there spending the summers fishing, hunt-ing, gathering food, and getting out of the heat of the valley just like tourists do today," Janetski said.

Tension built when white settlers moved in about 1870. Fish Lake was a sacred and spiritual god that furnished food for the Paiute Tribal Nation. Livestock trampling these hunting and ceremonial grounds resulted in the Black Hawk War. A treaty ending the fracas gave whites use of the waters forever. Paiutes received nine horses, 500 pounds of flour, one good beef steer and a suit of clothes.

Cattle and sheep still graze the hills in the summer. And at least one sheepherder left his mark. When Lorenzo Larsen grew bored while watch-ing sheep, he built stone monuments. Rock piles looking like dogs, tea kettles, and a woman with a frying pan still stand on the skylines near the first two miles of the Fish Lake road from Highway 24, said Rell G. Francis, who made a film about the sheepherder before Larsen died three years ago.

"He didn't like rocks under his feet," said Francis. "So where Lorenzo camped, he collected the rocks and made these 3- to 6-foot-high monuments. No mortar or connecting substance was used. He would pile up rocks and push little rocks in places to stabilize everything."

Most of Larsens monuments are of lava, a prevalent rock here. Volcanoes and erosion created this high country, just as it made all plateaus in central Utah, said Tom Abbay, geologist for the Salt Lake USDA Forest Service of-fice. Cliffs or talus slopes ring the 12-mile long, two-miles wide undulating mesa that stands 2,600 feet above Fish Lake. Since the area is "dull" geologi-cally—it has no spectacular features or mining possibilities—it is fairly un-known, Abbay continued. Lava probably welled up out of cracks and covered the area about 10 to 30 million years ago. Then came the water.

"Something caused the streams to occupy their present position and the water ate into the surrounding rock," Abbay said. "Eventually something had to be the last thing standing."

That something was Fish Lake Hightop. And on the west-northwest wall of this plateau sits the high point at 11,633 feet. To the north, Mt. Nebo can be seen on a clear day. The Tuschar mountains, with dominant peaks Mounts Belknap and Baldy, are southwest.

Mountain bikers, hikers, and equestrians make Fish Lake Hightop their domain. Managed like a wilderness area, motorized vehicles are forbidden in this high country, said Max Reid, recreation specialist on the Fishlake National Forest.

However, at the lake, three resorts and seven campgrounds lodge visitors who cast into some of the best fishing waters in Utah. For those who prefer watching wildlife, deer, elk and bear roam nearby. And osprey fly overhead searching for fish, said Ken McDonald, non-game biologist for the Division of Wildlife Resource's southern regional office.

Osprey migrate to Fish Lake from Central and South America where they spend winters. When hunting, they circle low over bodies of water looking for prey.

"When an osprey finds a fish, it folds its wings and plows into the water," McDonald said.

Utah Prairie Dogs, a threatened species, were introduced in an exclosure

North of Fish Lake Hightop, Sevier County's highest peak, the country is high, rolling hills. Paula Huff

near Pelican Point. This fenced coral still stands, but the burrowing squirrels could not make Fish Lake their home.

"Prairie dogs dig down 6 to 9 feet and the water table was just too high in the exclosure," McDonald said. "We also found the badgers were causing havoc." A transplant on nearby Parker Mountain was successful. And moose introduced to Fish Lake two years ago have found it suits their taste.

"Last fall I was at Pelican Point looking at the mist rising from the lake when this big bull moose came swimming across," said McDonald. "It was a National Geographic moment."

— *Paula Huff*

18   SUMMIT COUNTY — GILBERT PEAK

Summit:	13,442 ft.
Difficulty:	Difficult.
USGS maps:	Mt. Powell, Kings Peak.
Length:	9.5 miles.

Trailhead: From Evanston, Wyoming, drive east on Interstate 80 to Fort Bridger, about 35 miles. Get off the freeway at Fort Bridger and head east, then south to Mountain View. Drive south on Highway 414 for about 22 miles to Lonetree. Watch for a closed gas station on the right side of the road. Turn right after the station and follow the signs to Henrys Fork. From the parking lot, hike 8 miles to Dollar Lake. After Dollar Lake, there is no trail toward Gilbert Peak. On the east side of Dollar Lake, a ridge begins a quick ascent south. Climb this ridge and follow it until it intersects with another ridge that runs in a more east-west direction. Turn east and walk toward the saddle between Gunsight Peak and Gunsight Pass to the right/ south and Gilbert Peak to the left/north. From here, the route winds up the gentle, talus slopes of Gilbert Peak, which is marked with cairn.

The hike: Cars packed the Henry's Fork trailhead on the North Fork of the Uintas on a late summer weekend. A parade of backpackers, dogs, horses, and scout troops departed from there on their way to Kings Peak.

"That's our mountain freeway," quipped Mountain View Ranger District clerk Yvonne Lamb. "There are more people on that trail than there are on I-80."

There is a certain magic to climbing 13,528-foot Kings Peak, the tallest point in Utah. But 13,442-foot Gilbert Peak—the highest point in Summit County and the second tallest in Utah—sits 3.5 miles northeast of King's. With no trail and little notoriety, it gets largely ignored.

Lee Wickel, who worked eight summers as a USDA Forest Service wilderness ranger, hiked to the cairn-marked summit of Gilbert Peak four times.

SUMMIT COUNTY — GILBERT PEAK

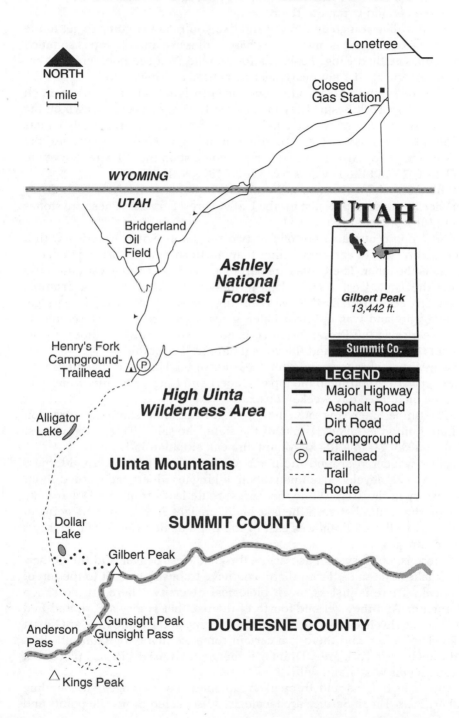

Lonetree

Closed
Gas Station

WYOMING

UTAH

Bridgerland
Oil
Field

Ashley
National
Forest

UTAH

*Gilbert Peak
13,442 ft.*

Summit Co.

Henry's Fork
Campground-
Trailhead

LEGEND
—	Major Highway
—	Asphalt Road
—	Dirt Road
△	Campground
Ⓟ	Trailhead
----	Trail
.....	Route

High Uinta
Wilderness Area

Alligator
Lake

Uinta Mountains

Dollar
Lake

SUMMIT COUNTY

Gilbert Peak

Anderson
Pass

△ Gunsight Peak
Gunsight Pass

DUCHESNE COUNTY

△ Kings Peak

Once, he saw no one. On another occasion, he was greeted by a troop of 40 girls. Like most hikers who make the trek, the false summits leading to the top proved a mild irritant to the ranger.

"It seems like you go on forever and like you're never going to get to the top," he said. "Gilbert is massive. Its base is massive and the top is so much more massive than Kings Peak. It's formidable. You see boulders that are the size of trucks. It's not nearly as fragmented as Kings Peak."

From the summit, hikers look down on Gunsight Peak and can see much of the Henry's Fork Basin. They look across to Kings Peak and down on the Atwood Basin, where Atwood Lake, the largest lake in the High Uintas Wilderness Area, is located. According to the book *Utah Place Names*, the peak is named for Grove Karl Gilbert, a geologist on the Wheeler Survey of 1871 to 1875 and the Powell survey from 1875 to 1879.

"Gilbert is made primarily of Precambrian quartzite and shale," said Barry Burkhardt, mineral specialist for the USDA Forest Service. "These are stones so old they predate fossils."

The Uinta Mountains are one of two ranges in North America with a general direction of east-west rather than north-south. The Brooks Range in Alaska is the other. The Uintas are part of a series of erosion-resistant rocks called the Uinta-Cortez arch. This formation wouldn't move or crumble when this section of Earth began shifting eastward millions of years go. Instead, the land was uplifted. Later, glaciers pushed younger sediments down, exposing the Precambrian core. So, when looking at Gilbert today, the old rocks sit on top and the younger are in the foothills.

Ivan Weber, of the newly formed Friends of the Uintas, is one hiker who looks forward to getting to the top of Gilbert and Kings, summits which can be done on a three-day weekend trip.

"The timberline is low enough there that I can understand the attraction of hiking into the highest peaks of the state," he said. "This is the nearest thing you can get to a Rocky Mountain peak situation in Utah."

As he wandered around the north slope of the Uintas as a wilderness ranger, Wickel developed opinions about hiking to Gilbert and learned about the history of the area. While the easiest route leads from the Dollar Lake area up the chutes between the lake and Gunsight Pass, he prefers going in from less well-used drainages east of the popular Red Castle and Henry's Fork drainages.

"There is a trail system accessible through West Beaver and the Gilbert Creek lakes," he said. "From there, you have to bushwhack it to the top of the peak. There is just as much biological diversity. There are no sheep allotments. And they get one-fourth of the use that Henry's Fork and Red Castle get." He once saw five bull moose grazing at the same time at Gilbert Lake. The ranger said there is a certain romance involving Gunsight Pass and the Henry's Fork area. Drainages merge at Gunsight Pass, a place that always seems windy and wild.

American Indians and trappers frequented the drainages surrounding Gilbert Peak. Forest Service archaeologists discovered projectile points and

The ridgeline leading to Gilbert Peak, Summit County's highest, has wonderful views of Kings Peak, far right, and Gunsight Peak, left. Gilbert Peak is not pictured here. Paula Huff

chipping sites around some lakes. One speculated the big rocks between Blanchard and Bear lakes were used to hide American Indian hunters while others pushed animals toward them. Burial sites have been discovered above Henry's Fork Lake. Upstream from Elkhorn Crossing along the Henry's Fork River, settlers built a sawmill just after the turn of the century. The river was used to float logs downstream to Granger, Wyoming.

"The boiler and grillwork are still there," reported Wickel. "The stack to the boiler is there and so are some flywheels. There was a fire on the side hill and the settlers never did rebuild the area."

A few old sheepherder cabins can be seen in the area below Gilbert Peak. And Wickel answered more than one complaint from backpackers who wondered what sheep were doing grazing in the Henry's Fork area, one of the few Uintas drainages where that practice is still allowed.

"Historically, the sheep were here before the wilderness act so ranchers still have grazing privileges as long as they follow guidelines and take care of their allotment," said the ranger. "I've never had to pick up a pop can or a gum wrapper from a sheep. You never see them cutting trees down like people do. People can condemn the sheep for being up there, but people have had more impact than sheep here in the last 100 years."

The presence of domestic sheep has precluded the Rocky Mountain bighorn which historically roamed the Uintas from multiplying in Henry's Fork. But they were reintroduced into the range seven years ago. Wickel

91

saw a ewe and lamb in the Henry's Fork Basin six years ago and a ram in the Middle Beaver range three years ago. There are a few mountain goats in the Red Castle area and pine marten and mountain lion are increasing.

Elk and moose are also common. In fact, moose are so common that hikers need to be aware of their presence and stay away from cows with calves, especially early in the hiking season which begins early in July and lasts until mid- to late September.

— Tom Wharton and Paula Huff

19   TOOELE COUNTY — DESERET PEAK

Summit:	11,031 ft.
Difficulty:	Moderate.
USGS maps:	Deseret Peak East, Deseret Peak West.
Length:	3.25 miles.

Trailhead: To reach the trailhead, drive to Grantsville. Driving west on Grantsville's main street, look for a large brown sign pointing to South Willow Canyon and Wasatch-Cache National Forest recreation areas. Follow signs to South Willow Canyon. The road turns into an easily accessible (for two-wheel drive vehicles) gravel road at the forest boundary. Take road to the end and park at a trailhead at the top of the road. An obvious sign across from the parking area leads to Deseret Peak trail.

There is a 3,900-foot elevation gain, making this a moderately difficult hike, but one that most hikers in reasonable condition should be able to enjoy.

The hike: Driving toward Grantsville on the edge of the Great Salt Lake desert, 16-year-old Texas transplant Lukas Staks couldn't imagine that he would soon be visiting a land of aspen and pines, mule deer, rattlesnakes, and wildflowers. The surprise came when the young hiker entered South Willow Canyon and began preparing to hike to 11,031-foot-high Deseret Peak at the end of the road. Like most people, Staks couldn't believe that such an oasis of green existed in the midst of the Great Basin desert.

Though many Wasatch Front hikers have discovered the joys of a visit to the highest point in Tooele County, most still savor the place because of its relative solitude. Salt Lake City resident Mark Hengesbaugh backpacks or hikes into the 25,500-acre Deseret Peak Wilderness Area at least once every year. After he leaves the trail, the hiker finds few people and many symbols of wilderness.

"We found a large rattler on the trail," he said while enjoying the view from the top of the peak. "It didn't move away, but it had enough energy to rattle so we were warned away."

TOOELE COUNTY — DESERET PEAK

NORTH

1 mile

Exit 99

TOOELE COUNTY

36

Exit 84

80

138

Flux

To Interstate 80

1 mile

138

36

South Willow Canyon sign →

Grantsville

North Willow Canyon

Tooele

Stansbury Mountains

South Willow Canyon

Stockton

Deseret Peak Wilderness

Ⓟ

Wasatch-Cache National Forest

UTAH

Deseret Peak

Trail 036

Antelope Canyon

Trail 044

LEGEND
— Major Highway
— Asphalt Road
— Dirt Road
△ Campgrounds
Ⓟ Trailhead
---- Trail

Deseret Peak
11,031 ft.

Tooele Co.

Salt Lake hiker Sabrine Pasquier found her heart pounding after sliding down a steep snowbank on a saddle near the summit. Even in mid-July, deep snow blocked access to the main trail, forcing hikers to take a steeper route.

Tooele resident Charlie Roberts makes the 6.5-mile-round-trip hike often. At one time, he celebrated Independence Day by taking his scout troop to the summit in the middle of the night.

"The trail is easily seen with a full moon or a flashlight," said Roberts. "I like to get to the summit and watch the sun rise over the Wasatch. It's spectacular."

Most hikers start the trek to the peak by driving to the end of South Willow Canyon, parking at a trailhead at the top of Loop Campground. Parking there is free, but a $5.00 charge is levied on vehicles parked in campsite pullouts. The hike begins in the shade of quaking aspens. A sign marks the start of the trail. Less than a half-block into the walk, a large wooden sign tells hikers they have entered the Deseret Peak Wilderness Area.

Clean, clear, snow-fed water feeds a stream which flows over yellow-colored rocks. Hikers ford the stream once, using some well-placed rocks to make the crossing. Right after the crossing, look for a sign marking a crossroads. Left goes to Deseret Peak, right to South Willow Lake.

"If you just go to the top of the loop and hike a mile or so, you can see some damage and carving of trees," said Roberts. "Once you get past the first mile or so and you cross the creek, you get away from all the wood carvings."

From there, the trail begins to switchback, continuing uphill into Douglas fir and other conifers. Close to the top of a saddle, trees begin to get more sparse and the view of the Great Salt Lake and the desert which surrounds it begins to open up. Hikers find themselves in a cirque-like natural amphitheater with steep cliffs. The trail leads up through rocks, wildflowers and tall grass to a saddle.

At that point, hikers can go south and then west to Bear Fork or north to Deseret Peak. The walk to the summit is normally an easy traverse, but in some years snow lingers longer than usual, forcing hikers to improvise a bit in an effort to rejoin the trail on the west side of the peak. A small man-made rock wind shelter is located near the summit, but there is no other visible sign that hikers are on top of Tooele County other than the views of the Great Salt Lake, Mt. Nebo on the Wasatch Front, and the Bonneville Salt Flats.

Hikers can turn back and take the same route down. Most, however, complete a loop hike by continuing down the trail on the west side of the summit. The trail is along the ridge, for the most part. There are three ways on this side of the mountain to make a descent. The trails are not as obvious or as well marked. Look for descents at each of the three saddles along the ridge.

According to Becky Hylland, a geological tecnhician at the Utah Geological Survey, rock exposed at the top of Deseret Peak is tintic quartzite, which

These two peaks can be seen from the summit of Deseret Peak, far left. Tom
Wharton

was deposited between 500 and 570 million years ago during the Cambrian
era when Utah was covered by a sea.

"Faulting began 15 million years ago, creating the basin and range topog-
raphy which is seen now," she said. "The Stansbury Mountains [where
Deseret Peak is located] are part of that basin and range. They are tilted
fault blocks of Mountains which can be commonly seen. The upper reaches
of the range did have glaciers in the Pleistocene, 10,000 to 1.6 million years
ago when the Stansburys were an island in Lake Bonneville. There were
glaciers on the northeast and south side, creating two glacial valleys."

The first humans to use the area were likely the Fremonts followed by
the Goshutes. According to the *Utah Historical Quarterly*, James McBride
and Harrison Severe identified the presence of Indians around Grantsville
in 1851. Writing in the *Quarterly's* 1987 edition, Steven Crum said the tribe
regarded Grantsville settler William Lee as a life-long friend. The Indians
made it clear to him that they had an inseparable relationship to their home-
land. They stated: "The Mountains are ours; the water, the woods, the grass,
the game all belong to us." These days, the area is managed by the Wasatch-
Cache National Forest.

Grantsville resident Ruth Matthews says pioneers like the Donner-Reed
party used the Stansbury Mountains and Deseret Peak more as a landmark
than anything else. The ill-fated party skirted the edge of the Mountains in
1846. Historian Jay Haymond speculated that a pioneer named Deseret Peak.

"The pioneers were probably working and using the land and they probably called it Deseret for industry because of that hard work," he said.

The peak sits in the mountains, named after Captain Howard Stansbury who was sent to survey the Great Salt Lake area in 1850. There was some mining activity in the range in the late 1800s, but Deseret Peak hikers will see little evidence of it.

The Wasatch Mountain Club staged a 1924 expedition that involved an all-night drive that ended when the transportation being used broke down. Private cars carried the gear and most club members walked to the trailheads.

"Once I sat down to rest, but the thoughts of Mountain lions and bears were too vivid to afford me any degree of relaxation so I continued on," wrote Alta Overmeyer about the trip. "After four miles of hiking and 50 minutes, I reached camp. The fire was crackling and the coffee boiling and everyone seemed happy. By 12:15, all had arrived and we were soon settled for the night. The prospective event of the day was the climb of Mt. Deseret, but, would you believe it, only eight of that hiking crowd made the attempt. I don't know whether it was a credit to me or not but I was the only girl so inclined. After an interminable climb, fraught with more or less danger and a little hard work, we arrived at our goal, the summit of Mt. Deseret."

The 45-minute trip to South Willow Canyon is easier these days. And many more folks trek to the peak. But some things never change.

"We gazed and gazed until we knew that the sun was beginning to hang low, then we decided to make the descent," wrote Overmeyer. "In two hours, I was back at camp. At Grantsville, we stopped and ate entirely too many ice cream cones."

— Tom Wharton

20   UTAH COUNTY — MT. NEBO

Summit:	11,928 ft.
Difficulty:	Difficult.
USGS maps:	Nebo Basin, Mona.
Length:	3.5 miles.

Trailhead: From Main Street in Payson, turn left on 100 North, then right on 600 East (Peteetneet Drive). This road turns into 2900 West and goes up Payson Canyon. Drive 26 miles to the White Pine/Nebo Bench trailhead. At the car park there is a road labeled Whitepine Hollow Trail, Santaquin Canyon, and Catkin Trail. Drive or walk this road to the cattleguard. At the cattleguard begin following a barbed-wire fence to the left. This fence ends at a knoll. Look northwest for another barbed wire fence. This fence is build along a subsidiary ridge that leads to the main Mt. Nebo peak ridgeline. Follow this new fence, and when it ends, continue west on a faint trail to the main Mt. Nebo ridgeline. Once you connect with the Mt. Nebo ridgeline, follow it south past North Peak, Wolf Pass, then climb a steep, long talus slope to Mt. Nebo's north peak.

UTAH COUNTY — MOUNT NEBO

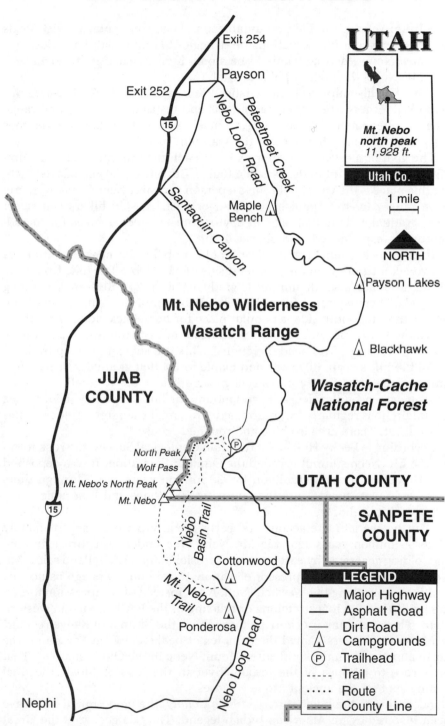

This is a very difficult hike because of steep climbs, talus with exposure, and faint trails

The hike: Veteran Salt Lake mountaineer and environmental activist Alexis Kelner craves solitude, something he struggles to find in Salt Lake County's canyons. Now, when he wants to be alone, Kelner heads south to 11,928-foot Mt. Nebo, the highest point in Utah County.

"I love its high alpine characteristics," Kelner said of the 28,170-acre Mt. Nebo Wilderness Area. "The panoramas and vistas of the basin and range area are phenomenal. Nebo still has a nice wildness to it that is sometimes disappearing from other parts of the Wasatch."

The goal of most Nebo explorers is to reach the mountain's north summit, the highest point in the Wasatch Range. But one of the appeals to reaching this place is the variety of routes a person can take. Kent Cornaby, recreation ranger for the Spanish Fork Ranger District, said hikers can select long, gradual ascents that take all day or shorter, steeper hikes for the adventurous, experienced, and physically fit.

If there is a "main" trailhead, it would probably be near the Andrews Canyon campground on the southeast side of Mt. Nebo. The hike from here to the mountain's south summit is gradual but, at 21 miles, makes a long day trek. There is access from the Nebo Bench trail that runs across from the north to the south side, a popular place for horseback riders. And there is Willow Creek, accessed from a road heading east from the Juab County town of Mona (see Trailhead directions). This is a short, but steep trail.

All the hikes begin in an oak and maple forest that gradually turns into a timbered area and finally into a rocky, barren slope above treeline.

"You can encounter deer, elk, and mountains lions, though you won't see mountain lions regularly," Cornaby said. "You might see some golden eagles or a bobcat. There are also blue and roughed grouse."

According to Becky Hylland of the Utah Geological Survey, the rock forming the Mt. Nebo summit is called the Oquirrh Formation. It was deposited as sediment in a sea 290 million to 330 million years ago. Through time, these sediments turned into the quartzites, siltstones and limestones seen today on Mt. Nebo.

"During the late Cretaceous and early Tertiary periods—approximately 55 to 96 million years ago—the Mt. Nebo area underwent thrust faulting and folding generated by east-west compressional forces," Hylland said. "Mt. Nebo began to attain its present elevation 15 million years ago as normal faulting began along the Wasatch Fault. Now, instead of compression forces, the faulting is due to a stretching or relaxing of the Earth's crust in western Utah. This stretching is occurring throughout the Basin and Range region."

Mormon pioneers named the complex of peaks between Payson on the north and Nephi on the south after Mount Nebo in the Old Testament. That peak rose to the east of the Jordan River in the land of Moab, the final resting spot for the ancient prophet Moses.

According to the book *History of Juab County*, the name might also have been inspired by an American Indian legend. The tale goes that the Great

Hikers walk the ridgeline leading to the north peak of Mt. Nebo, Utah County's highest peak. Paula Huff

Spirit Wakunda asked that an ancient princess named Nebona be sacrificed to atone for a mistake her father made. The women's fiancee, Running Deer, was told this by an eagle while on the peak. After much praying and persuasion, Running Deer persuaded Wakunda to spare Nebona. As he raced to the summit of the peak to stop Nebona, he watched in horror as she hurled herself off the peak. Unthinking, Running Deer followed her off the cliff.

Wakunda, who felt sorry for his children, took them into the heart of his mountain, where they sleep to this day waiting for someone to unlock their chamber. The Great Spirit named the mountain Mount Nebo in honor of the princess who gave her life for her people.

The *History of Juab County* also revealed several other interesting historical facts about the mountain:

• The first record of pioneers ascending the mountain was made by W. W. Phelps, who reached the summit on Aug. 24, 1869, to make scientific observations.

• Lieutenant George M. Wheeler of the U.S. Topographical Survey erected an observatory on its summit after he and several men carved a trail to the top so they could carry lumber up on mules.

• In 1881, a Coast and Geodetic Survey station was established to help determine a parallel across the country. The Coast and Geodetic Survey was operated by the U.S. Department of Commerce until two years ago, when it was eliminated. It performed a similar function to the U.S. Geologic Survey in terms of mapping. A triangle consisting of Mt. Baldy, Mt. Jeff Davis—now Wheeler Peak in Great Basin National Park—and Nebo was established.

Lines were formed as signals were flashed with mirrors three times a day.

While canyons such as Santaquin and Payson were used by local residents for camping, picnicking, fishing, and some water storage, much of the east side of Mt. Nebo remained wild until the 1930s, when the Civilian Conservation Corps established a primitive dirt road stretching from Payson Canyon to Salt Creek Canyon east of Nephi.

"In the early 1980s, that road was paved," Cornaby said. "Before, there was a rough two-track road. It took drivers three hours to drive from Nephi to Payson Lake."

The road, now a popular scenic drive that includes several nice campgrounds, many horseback trails, a red-rock formation known as Devils Kitchen, and the well-used Payson Lakes camping and fishing complex, is called the Nebo Loop. Thousands enjoy fall and summer drives along the scenic mountain road. On a fall day, when the top of Mt. Nebo is dusted with the season's first snowfall, many enjoy the contrast of blue sky, white snow on a treeless peak and the reds, yellows, and oranges of changing leaves lower in the canyon.

The peak's steep slopes and rugged terrain leave it wild. And that keeps those who love the Wasatch happy.

— Tom Wharton

21   WASATCH COUNTY — UNNAMED PEAK (PROPOSED NAME—MT. CARDWELL)

Summit:	10,743 ft.
Difficulty:	Easy.
USGS map:	Mirror Lake.
Length:	1.25 miles.

Trailhead: On the Mirror Lake Road, State Highway 150, park at milepost 28. There is a dirt road and turnout for parking on the north side. There is no trail. Cross the road and walk in a south-by-southeast direction. Trees thin and a talus ridge appears to the east. Get on this ridge and follow it to the peak, marked by a 7-foot cairn.

Wasatch County is one of two Utah counties that has a point higher than the tallest peak. Near Wasatch's highest peak a ridgeline leads to Murdock Mountain. Before exiting the county, this ridge reaches 10,840 feet.

The hike: As a teenager, John Clegg strapped 5-gallon milk jugs on either side of a horse, filled them with water, added a chunk of ice, some live fish, and hauled the cargo to lakes surrounding Wasatch County's highest peak.

"That's why I always knew where the best fishing would be," boasted Clegg, a retired Brigham Young University electrical engineering professor.

WASATCH COUNTY — UNNAMED PEAK

UTAH

Unnamed Peak
10,743 ft.

Wasatch Co.

SUMMIT COUNTY

Ashley National Forest

Mt. *Agassiz*

Mirror Lake

Highline Trail

Mirror Lake

Moose Lake

Bald Mountain

Uinta Mountains

Lilly Lake

Trial Lake

Lost Creek

(P)

Bald Mountain

DUCHESNE COUNTY

150

Echo Lake

Wasatch County's unnamed high peak

Pyramid Lake

Upper Provo River

Mirror Lake Highway

To Kamas

WASATCH COUNTY

LEGEND

——	Asphalt Road
△	Campground
(P)	Car Park
....	Route
▨▨▨	County Line

1 mile

Fish planting is quite different today. Every week a Division of Wildlife Resources airplane skims the surface of lakes on the southwest corner of the Uinta Mountains, dropping brook and cutthroat trout as it passes. Clegg no longer predicts angling hot spots for Trial, Lost, Pyramid, Blizzard or Echo lakes, which surround Wasatch County's high point. But this country still cradles his heart and may soon carry a family name.

Wasatch County's 10,743-foot-high peak is unnamed. A contest sponsored by the *Salt Lake Tribune* proposes the moniker Mt. Cardwell, after Clegg's father, Henry Cardwell Clegg. Most knew him as Cardie. For more than five decades, Cardie built dams and tended 15 reservoirs around Trial Lake. He released the water for irrigation and culinary use in Kamas, Heber, Provo, and Salt Lake City. A two-story cabin on Trial Lake's west shore became a summer home for Cardie and his family. Memories built there for 40 years. Those stories still get passed around relatives' campfires.

Cardie made more than 30 winter trips near Wasatch County's highest peak to conduct snow surveys. Before snowmobiles, he strapped snowshoes to his feet and walked 60 miles round trip. Shelter was a snow cave. Provisions were rolled in a blanket and flung over his shoulder, since vandals usually absconded with any food left in the cabin.

One year, after thieves stole goods from the summer home, Cardie and his partner made a half loaf of bread last four days, according to Cardie's wife, Marion, in her autobiography, *My Life on Trial*.

"We tried to scare up some meat," Cardie told Marion. "We did get a squirrel, and each of us ate a bite. We also killed a porcupine and boiled it for two days trying to get it tender enough to eat. But we couldn't swallow it."

There just isn't much food in this high country, which is near tree line. Even American Indians, using this as a summer-hunting area as long as 8,000 years ago, had to be creative. On scree-covered slopes like Wasatch County's high peak, Indians made indentations by moving rocks, said Kelda Malmstrom, archaeological technician with the Ashley National Forest. One hunter hid in the rock depression while others below chased bighorn sheep toward him.

"Wildlife biologists say bighorn sheep run straight uphill when they are scared," Malmstrom said. "Someone in the blind would have killed them as they passed."

Connecting these rock depressions with American Indians is so new there is little information published, Malmstrom continued. That is changing. When American Indians moved the rocks, lichen on the stones was often placed in a direction it could never grow naturally. Archaeologists are beginning to use this multicolored growth to date the sites.

Rocks moved by American Indians were primarily Precambrian quartzite and shale, stones so old they predate fossils, said Barry Burkhardt, mineral specialist for the USDA Forest Service. On a larger scale, these rocks are part of the Uinta μountains, one of two ranges in North America with a general direction of east-west rather than north-south. The Brooks Range in Alaska is the other.

Wasatch County's highest peak is marked by a huge cairn. Paula Huff

Uinta Mountain peaks are related to erosion-resistant rocks called the Uinta-Cortez arch. This formation wouldn't move or crumble when the earth began shifting eastward millions of years ago. Instead, the land was up-lifted. Later in the Uintas, glaciers pushed younger sediments downward, exposing the Precambrian core. So when looking at these peaks today, the old rocks sit on top and the young in the foothills.

Pine marten, elk, deer, moose, black bear, cougar, coyotes, and fox live among these peaks. Two of the more unique animals that can be spotted are mountain goats and pica. And there are wolves, according to Calvin Giles, who now works Cardie's job.

"I told some guys I had seen wolves, but they didn't believe me," said Giles, who now roams Wasatch County's highest peak on horseback. "But we were eating dinner once near this pile of dirt about 40 feet high. We heard this mournful cry. We looked up and those wolves were standing on top of that pile of dirt howling. I saw them again last year."

This man, who considers himself a modern-day Daniel Boone, has also watched two male bobcats fight over a female. The felines would jump in the air, clawing each other, and howling. These sightings are becoming more rare. Trial Lake now sees 3,000 anglers on holiday weekends. And Highway 150, the main road near Wasatch County's highest peak, has summer traffic jams.

"But in the fall, when the people are gone and all the animals are at a lower elevation, it's so quiet I can hear the squeak of the pines."

— Paula Huff

Summit:	10,365 ft.
Difficulty:	Moderate.
USGS map:	Signal Peak.
Length:	4 miles from Oak Creek; 5 miles from Brown's Point.

Trailhead: For the Oak Grove trail, exit Interstate 15 at Leeds, exit 23. Turn west onto the Silver Reed Road. Follow signs along this road to the Oak Grove Campground, about a 9-mile drive. Park at the trailhead in the campground. This is a hot, steep route during summer months. Follow a well-defined trail that goes to the Pine Valley Mountain ridgeline, a 3-mile walk. Drop over the ridge—still following a path—until reaching a sign that says Whipple Lake/Oak Grove Campground/Further Water, about 0.25 mile from the ridge. Take the Further Water trail, headed west. At this point the trail is called Summit Trail on maps. Walk this trail to the Squaw Canyon drainage (no sign) where another trail joins from the north. The trail turns south through a high alpine meadow, then west where the path begins traversing Signal Peak. The trail does not ascend Signal Peak. Begin bushwacking south 0.25 mile to the summit, where there is a small cairn, and register.

For the Browns Point Trail, drive to the Pine Valley Campground on the north side of the Pine Valley Mountains. Follow signs to the Browns Point Trailhead. Walk the well-defined Browns Point Trail as it climbs the north face of the Pine Valley Mountains, goes over a ridge and drops into Nay Canyon, about 4 miles. At this point a sign says South Valley/Whipple Valley/Browns Point. Continue south along the Browns Point trail, which ascends the Nay Canyon drainage. In about 0.75 mile, there is a sign that reads Whipple Lake/Oak Grove Campground/Further Water. From this sign—the same named in the Oak Grove Campground trail—use directions from above to reach Signal Peak. Thick trees and rolling hills make Signal Peak difficult to find. A map and compass are necessary.

The hike: While hiking from the depths of southwestern Utah's desert to 10,365-foot Signal Peak—the highest point in Washington County—trekkers view one of the state's most lush and diverse forests.

"One of the things that make the Pine Valley Mountains unique is the diversity of their plant species," said Fred Ybright, the USDA Forest Service's coordinator for the 50,000-acre wilderness area on the range. "We have a small stand of bristlecone pine near Burger Peak. There are Engleman spruce, Douglas fir, limber pine, pinyon pine, ponderosa pine, junipers, mountain mahogany, and serviceberry. We go from the yucca and cholla of the desert to aspen and subalpine communities. The wildflowers are quite abundant. It's almost parklike."

There is a primeval feel in this quiet wilderness. Three-inch-thick humus

WASHINGTON COUNTY — SIGNAL PEAK

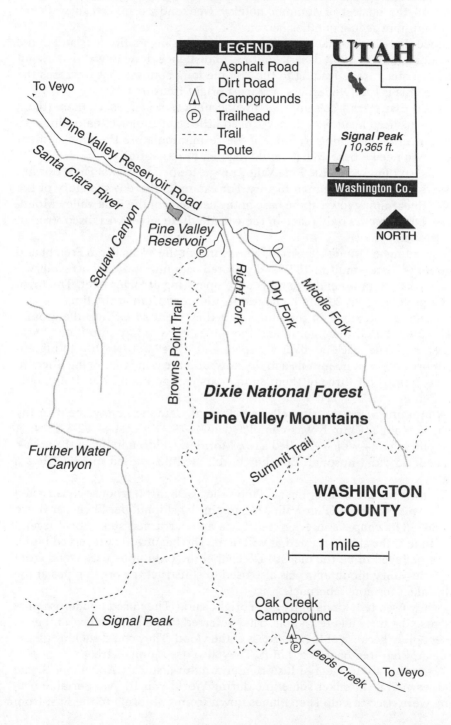

LEGEND
— Asphalt Road
— Dirt Road
⚠ Campgrounds
Ⓟ Trailhead
--- Trail
···· Route

UTAH

Signal Peak
10,365 ft.

Washington Co.

NORTH

To Veyo

Pine Valley Reservoir Road

Santa Clara River

Squaw Canyon

Pine Valley Reservoir Ⓟ

Right Fork

Dry Fork

Middle Fork

Browns Point Trail

Dixie National Forest

Pine Valley Mountains

Further Water Canyon

Summit Trail

WASHINGTON COUNTY

1 mile

⚠ Signal Peak

Oak Creek Campground

⚠ Ⓟ

Leeds Creek

To Veyo

covers much of the forest bottom. Only the wind and the occasional explosion of a forest grouse or chattering of a squirrel seem to break the silence. Even on the busiest of summer holiday weekends, a hiker can walk for miles without seeing another person.

Since there are no lakes and little water on this high-altitude island in the midst of southern Utah desert, solitude and silence draw a few visitors not afraid of steep trails leading to the 35-mile-long summit that traverses the peaks. This is true wilderness, a place Ybright treasures.

"Land managers," he said, "need wilderness as much [as] or more [than] physicians need healthy bodies. We need little strongholds of naturalness so we can have something to judge if we're manipulating the environment badly. We need a base. What would happen here naturally?"

This isn't to say that the Pine Valley range, topped by Signal Peak, doesn't possess a fascinating human history. For example, there is the story of the Silver Reef mining town at the base of the east side of the Pine Valley Mountains. That was the only place in the world where silver was discovered in sandstone.

According to Wanda Hausman, who works at the Wells Fargo Freight and Shipping Office—built in 1877 and restored as a museum and art gallery—there were 33 mines and five mills once operating at Silver Reef. The town had a population of 2,000, the largest in southern Utah at the time.

"There is still silver in the mines, but they went so far into the ground that water started to come up and there was no way to pump it out," said Hausman. "The price of silver dropped, and it was not worth it to mine it anymore. We have no mining activity now, and the mines are being filled in. We've capped off three of them so the bats can go in and out, but people can't enter."

A monument on the site tells the story of Catholic involvement in the area. St. John's Church was completed in 1879 at a cost of $2,372.14. A Catholic school—which enrolled a few Mormon children living in the area—opened. So did a hospital. But the church facilities closed in 1887 after a fire.

That wasn't the case for the old Pine Valley LDS meetinghouse constructed on the west side of the Pine Valley Mountains by shipbuilder Ebenezer Bryce in 1868. The chapel's interior resembles an overturned ship. Local legend says that, if the ship is righted, it will float. The beautifully preserved building is believed to be the oldest LDS chapel in continuous use. Wood from the Pine Valley mountains was also used to construct the organ pipes at the Salt Lake Mormon Tabernacle.

"They used two kinds of trees," Ybright said. "They used ponderosa pine because the trees had few knots. They referred to the Pine Valley lumber as 'sweet pine' because of the clearness of the wood. They could get long pieces of clear, knot-free boards out of it. They also used juniper trees."

According to St. George historian and naturalist Bart Anderson, Signal Peak earned its moniker sometime during World War II. Two portable beacons were used to help keep planes flown from California to the East from

The hike to Signal Peak, Washington County's highest, has wonderful views of cliffs and red rock country. Paula Huff

crashing into the tallest peaks. One was placed on Signal Peak.

The peak and the range that contains it are part of the largest laccolith in Utah. Salt Lake geologist Genevieve Atwood uses a familiar image to describe the geology that formed the range. She said a sedimentary mountain would resemble a newspaper-recycling bin with the oldest newspapers—or rocks in the case of the mountain—on the bottom and the youngest on top. The laccolith contains newer igneous rocks that extend out of the range like Christmas tree branches and are then exposed by erosion.

"It would be as if a teenage boy embarrassed about owning several new issues of Playboy magazine hid them in the midst of that stack of newspapers," Atwood said. "The igneous represented by the magazines would intrude between the layers of sedimentary rock."

To a casual observer, the rock on the steep hike to tree-covered Signal Peak looks like granite. But Atwood said that isn't an accurate description. She would call the rock light-colored, intrusive igneous rocks.

One thing is certain. The climb from the desert floor at 2,800 feet to the top of the 10,000-foot range is steep. Since the major trailheads at the Oak Grove Campground on the range's eastern side and the Pine Valley camping complex on the west side begin near the wilderness area, which begins at about 7,500 feet, hikers can expect a steep climb to the summit.

There is a good population of mule deer in the area, and an occasional cougar and rattlesnake can be seen. Cattle graze on 15,000 acres of the 50,000-acre wilderness.

It might take time and effort, but the best camping areas on the mountain are found in large meadows near the top.

— *Tom Wharton*

(Paula Huff also contributed to this story)

23 WAYNE COUNTY — BLUEBELL KNOLL

Summit:	11,320 ft.
Difficulty:	Easy.
USGS maps:	Government Point, Blind Lake.
Length:	0.25 mile.

Trailhead: From Blackburn's Sinclair in Bicknell, drive 2.5 miles east on Highway 24. Turn south onto a paved road. Drive to the Kings Ranch/Boulder Top sign, and take the right fork toward Boulder Top. The road soon turns to dirt. In about 3 miles, look for a sign at a fork that says Antelope Spring-Pollywog Lake right. Take the left fork. In less than a mile, there is another fork, where you must turn left again onto Forest Service Road 178. Drive until you reach snow. Using a detailed map, ski this dirt road to Bluebell Knoll. (A map is especially helpful on top, where the terrain is flat and nondescript when there is snow.) In the winter this road is not plowed after the King Ranch turnoff. A gate prevents motorized traffic from using it after Cook and Miller lakes. In the summer, you can drive a four-wheel drive to within feet of Bluebell Knoll.

The hike: "Aquarius Plateau should be described in blank verse and illustrated upon canvas."

That's how Charles E. Dutton began a government report in 1872 on the country hosting Wayne County's highest peak. Written for explorer/surveyor John Wesley Powell's *Geology of the High Plateaus of Utah*, Dutton departed from the severe ascetic scientific style to sculpt this jumbled landscape with torrid prose.

"The explorer who sits upon the brink of its parapet looking off into the southern and eastern haze, who skirts its lava-cap or clambers up and down its vast ravines, who builds his campfire by the borders of its snow-fed lakes or stretches himself beneath its giant pines and spruces, forgets that he is a geologist and feels himself a poet," he mused.

West of Capitol Reef National Park and between Bicknell and Boulder, a two-layered wedding cake helps one visualize this landscape. On the bottom tier is the Aquarius Plateau. On top—and scooted eastward—is a smaller tier, called Boulder Top or Boulder Mountain. And rising slightly from a road that circles its base is Bluebell Knoll, the tip-top of Wayne County's wonderland at 11,320 feet.

Back to Dutton.

"When the broad platform is gained the story of 'Jack and the Beanstalk,' the finding of a strange and beautiful country somewhere up in the region of the clouds, no longer seems incongruous. Yesterday, we were toiling over a burning soil, where nothing grows save the ashy-colored sage, the prickly pear, and a few cedars that writhe and contort their stunted limbs under a scorching sun. Today we are among forests of rare beauty and luxuriance;

the air is moist and cool, the grasses are green and rank, and hosts of flowers deck the turf like the hues of a Persian carpet."

Flat plain best describes Boulder Mountain and the Colorado Plateau millions of years ago. Lava flows formed a thick cap over the Boulder Mountain area, protecting it when erosion began. But all around, wind and rain tore away thousands of feet of sandstone, shale, and other rock, creating the maze-like Colorado Plateau.

After several ice ages, Aquarius' lava cap gave away slightly. Glaciers crumbled the edges, creating Boulder Mountain's retreating rim-rock cliffs. Volcanic rubble—in the form of rounded black rocks—still litters the red-rock foothills.

Four-wheelers know this country best now. Hundreds of miles of roads criss-cross its top, remnants of logging a plateau heralded as one of the highest evergreen forests in the world. Anglers visit too, since there are lakes and streams in every nook. Food brought the first people.

"There are American Indian sites completely surrounding Boulder Top. It is packed," said Craig Harmon, archaeologist for the Bureau of Land Management Richfield district. "At 10,000 feet are temporary hunting camps. Around 9,000 feet, you run into camps that have long-term use. The most interesting thing is the variety of stuff."

A tool made from a bison's jaw was found in a cave. These beefy animals vanished 10,000 years ago. About 700 years ago, the Fremont built stone walls to funnel pronghorn antelope into corrals made of brush. Points used for the slaughter still speckle the ground. Anasazi houses line cliff walls. Written records tell of the Navajo, Shoshone, and Piute.

Early rancher John King said wild game was plentiful, and constituted the main part of the Piutes' diet. Grass seed was gathered and ground into meal. But what American Indians saw as food, white settlers saw as cattle feed. Grass scraped cows bellies when Richfield residents first arrived in 1879 with their livestock. Horses and sheep were munching there soon. By 1904, Boulder Mountain fed 75,000 sheep and 12,500 cattle, said Lenora LeFevre in *Boulder Country and Its People*. Government intervention began.

"By 1900, ranges on Boulder Mountain were suffering from drought and overgrazing," says LeFevre. "By 1903, the once-rich meadows on the mountain had turned to dust beds."

Cowpunchers Amasa Mason Jr. and Rosannah Reynolds Lyman moved to the south side of Boulder Mountain on the West Fork of Boulder Creek in 1890. Home was a wagon cover strung between several trees, until a one-room cabin could be built.

Life on Boulder Mountain was hard work for Rosannah. She made laundry soap. Meat was cured and smoked or bottled in a pressure cooker. Vegetables and fruit were dried or canned. Homemade cheese and sauerkraut filled her family's plates. And with yeast made from a potato, she baked six to eight loaves of bread every other day.

To clothe nine children, Rosannah tanned animal skins, made them into gloves and traded her product in Escalante for calico. When times were

WAYNE COUNTY — BLUEBELL KNOLL

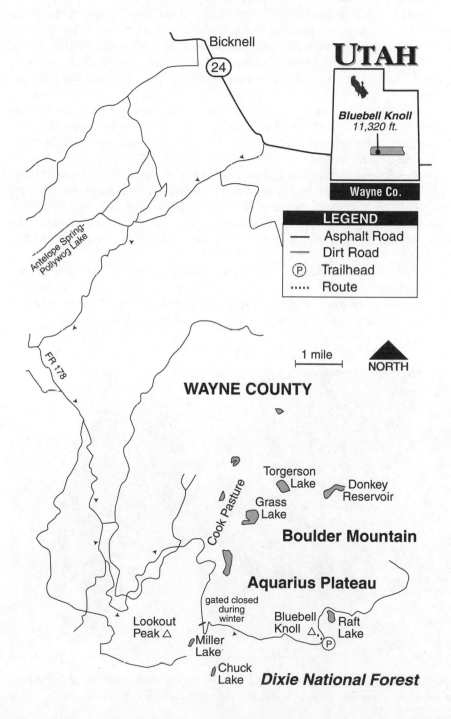

Bicknell

24

UTAH

Bluebell Knoll
11,320 ft.

Wayne Co.

LEGEND
— Asphalt Road
— Dirt Road
Ⓟ Trailhead
····· Route

Antelope Spring-Pollywog Lake

FR 178

1 mile

NORTH

WAYNE COUNTY

Torgerson
Lake

Donkey
Reservoir

Cook Pasture

Grass
Lake

Boulder Mountain

Aquarius Plateau

gated closed
during
winter

Lookout
Peak △

Bluebell
Knoll
△

Raft
Lake

Ⓟ

Miller
Lake

Chuck
Lake

Dixie National Forest

really rough, she cut up the wagon cover and sewed hats, jackets and pants for three boys, remembers her daughter, Maria Lyman King. The hard work never turned her sour on country living.

"Mother loved the outdoors," recalls her daughter Rhoda in the *King Chronicles*. "I can never remember Dad ever going hunting or fishing, but mother was known to be great at both sports. Mother loved to fish when they were living at Grass Valley Ranch. She would take us children with her and walk up to the creek which was several miles away to try her hand at fishing."

Aquarius Plateau trees had long ago been cut and used to build nearby homes. After a bark-beetle epidemic, logging Engelmann Spruce on Boulder Mountain began in earnest in the 1950s. Of course, that meant a road had to be plowed into the forest.

"My uncle and three other guys hired a county cat [and a driver] to bull-doze in a road along an old sheep trail," recalls Charlie Torgerson. "They filled that old boy up with wine, and when he would say that he didn't think he could get up there, they would give him some more wine. He finally got up there. He only lasted for a day and half, though. He got too spooked."

Most of the timber went to Carbon and Emery counties for mine props, says Marvin Turner, Teasdale district US Forest Service ranger. Two saw-mills logged on Boulder Mountain during the summer, and dozens sprang up around its circumference. Most have closed, but cutting continues, much

Bluebell Knoll, Wayne County's highest peak, has a road a matter of feet from its crest. A winter ski in makes the trip more challenging. Paula Huff

to Mark Clemens' consternation. As chair of the Utah Sierra Club's Utah Valley group, he hopes to stop proposed cutting five miles southwest of Bluebell Knoll in Jacob-Swale.

"There is no denying that Boulder Mountain is one of the most beautiful places on earth," Clemens said. "But it has been seen as nothing more than a fiber farm. These woods are less and less full of species that were fairly common. We want to see some of the species restored. May we succeed, and you live to see the first wolverine return to the area."

— Paula Huff

24 WEBER COUNTY — WILLARD PEAK

Summit:	9,764 ft.
Difficulty:	Moderate.
USGS maps:	Mantua, North Ogden.
Length:	7.25 miles.

Trailhead: From Interstate 15 take the 12th Street exit into Ogden. Head east on 12th Street until the intersection with Washington Blvd., then turn north. Stay on Washington Blvd. until the intersection with 3100 North. Turn east on 3100 North, which leads into North Ogden Canyon. At the North Ogden Canyon summit is a parking lot. The well-marked trail begins across the street from the car park. There is an alternative trailheads starting at the North Fork Park Campground north of Liberty.

The hike: Maybe it's because a plaque sits atop Ben Lomond. Maybe it's because Ben Lomond is more pointed, therefore more peak-like. Maybe it's because all trails lead to Ben Lomond. Perhaps it's because Ben Lomond served as the model for the Paramount Pictures logo. Willard is 47 feet taller, though.

Named after Willard Richards, a counselor to Mormon Church leader Brigham Young, this summit is a long, flat-topped rock outcropping. It is about one mile north of Ben Lomond on the same ridge line. The Great Salt Lake sits at its front door with sagebrush desert terrain sweeping up the west face to the peak. Its east-facing back door is lush with pines, thick groundcover and 28 varieties of wildflowers.

Because of the big body of water to the west, seagulls pinwheel overhead. Hikers reaching the top look down the backbone of the Wasatch, into Nevada, across Cache Valley to Idaho, and southeast to the Uintas. But signs of humans on every slope are the attention grabbers.

This peak's history is etched in its soil. American Indian trails were the first landmarks. Peter Skene Ogden, one of the first whites to enter the area, led trappers into Ogden Valley in 1825. He followed a well-worn path that began in Cache Valley, according to William W. Terry's *Weber County is Worth Knowing*. After trapping a few days, he led the brigade south over another trail to the Weber River at Mountain Green. Both trails are outlined on a granite plaque at the top of North Ogden Canyon today.

"This monument—the only one in the state of Utah that shows the Indians did something besides fight the white man—is impressive," said Terry.

On the "bold and rugged" west-facing cliffs of Willard where bighorn sheep once made their homes and eagles nested, Don Maguire of Ogden built a mine, according to *The Salt Lake Mining Review*. It was called Eldorado. The year was 1897.

Maguire built a precipitous donkey trail to the mine, which was supposedly rich in silver. Masonry walls connected cliffs hundreds of feet apart. Hanging bridges did the same. An aerial tramway—which still stands—was constructed to move the precious metal from about 9,000 feet down to the valley floor, according to Lee Groberg, an independent filmmaker who created KUED's *Treasure House: Utah's Mining Story*.

"Because of the steepness of the mountain side, this is an unusual mine," said Groberg. "I went in it two years ago. It was two feet deep in slimy ooze. I got out of it quick because it was a place you just didn't want to be."

By 1910, the mine that supposedly was going to "make everyone in Ogden rich" blipped from existence. Some believe Eldorado was a fraud to bilk eastern investors of money.

From 1901 to 1905, 205 tons of ore worth $996 was taken from Eldorado. The aerial tramway to move it cost $50,000. A mill for the ore cost $20,000. The mine that was supposedly thick with silver contained 40 percent lead, 3 percent zinc, three ounces of silver per ton, and a trace of gold.

"It was previously reported as containing, gold, silver, copper, lead, zinc, antimony, iron, nickel, cobalt, molybdenite, and uranium," writes Bruce Jessen in a thesis on Weber County mining. "This hoax was no more than a low-grade lead mine, totally unworthy of development."

Exploratory mining tunnels and shafts still pock the mountains east of Ogden. None are deep enough to have produced much, says Groberg. That's one reason cattle and sheep grazing reigned. Brigham Young warned Mormons away from the pursuit of precious metals. Agriculture and livestock were more important in a self-sustaining community, he said. And so, the mountains were grazed and timber was cut for homes "until there was nothing left," said lifelong Willard resident John Edwards in an oral history.

The timber harvesting and overgrazing contributed to a series of floods off Willard Peak. The first was August 13, 1923. Black, ominous clouds hung over the peak on that late Friday afternoon. By 8 P.M. it began to rain, turning into a downpour. Edwards compared it to "being under Niagara Falls."

"The roar was so terrific and the noise so great that you couldn't converse with anyone in the room," said Edwards. "...We didn't know whether the roof of the house was going to hold. My sister and I were under the kitchen table. We thought Armageddon had come...Mother was hollering at the top

WEBER COUNTY — WILLARD PEAK

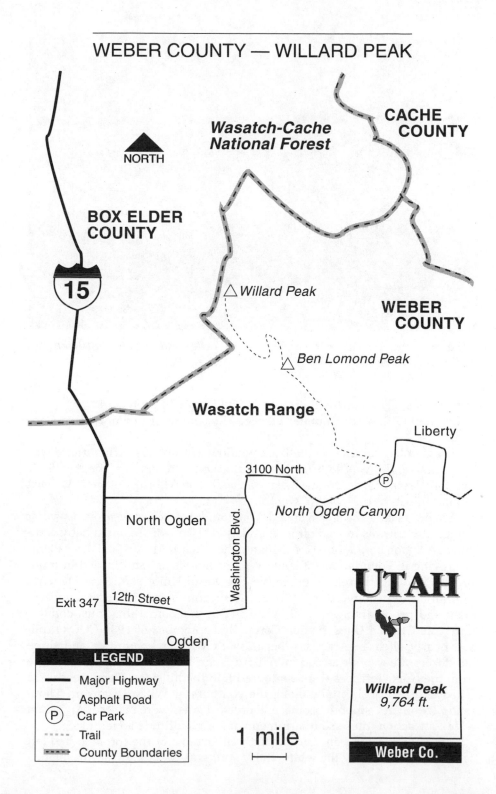

Wasatch-Cache National Forest

CACHE COUNTY

NORTH

BOX ELDER COUNTY

15

△ *Willard Peak*

WEBER COUNTY

△ *Ben Lomond Peak*

Wasatch Range

Liberty

3100 North

Ⓟ

North Ogden Canyon

North Ogden

Washington Blvd.

Exit 347 | 12th Street

Ogden

UTAH

Willard Peak
9,764 ft.

Weber Co.

LEGEND

▬▬▬	Major Highway
—	Asphalt Road
Ⓟ	Car Park
·····	Trail
▰▰▰	County Boundaries

1 mile

On a clear day, one can look over the Ogden Valley and into the Salt Lake Valley atop Weber County's highest peak - Willard. Paula Huff

of her voice, `The Lord will protect us, the Lord will protect us.' "

Lightening flashed. Thunder crashed. Rocks swept down Willard Canyon.

"I remember running to the back window of the house when there was lightening, and it was so bright you could see the mountain," he recalls. "I can only describe it as looking like a waterfall. The whole frontage of Willard Mountain was a solid wall of water."

Two hours later the storm ended. Water and debris had destroyed several homes. A barn was moved off its foundation. Two women and a baby were killed. A 50-ton boulder had crashed into the Willard Municipal Power Plant, destroying it. Foundations of some Willard homes are still buried in mud, says Teddy Griffith, retired executive director of Union Station in Ogden.

Another destructive storm July 31, 1936, convinced the federal government and people living around Willard Peak that something must change. Enter the Civilian Conservation Corps. By September of 1936 CCC enrollees, nearly all from Arkansas, began work with jackhammers and three bulldozers. They built a road in Willard Basin that ends about a half mile from the peak. Terraces were contoured into the hillsides. Dead trees were felled and laid horizontally along the contours of Willard Canyon. Thousands of conifers, smooth brome, and orchard grass were planted. And as an added attraction, these southern men got a high-altitude adventure.

Snow began falling on a Friday night after most of the foremen had left camp. By the next day the white, fluffy stuff was waist high, according to a

1969 interview with J. J. Wise of Ogden, supervisor of the crew. They kept brushing it off their tents to prevent their collapse. On Monday, the workers received orders to walk out the next morning. After a breakfast of frozen onions, the caravan of about 80 marched eight miles to a truck sent to retrieve them. After a partial thaw a few days later, they returned to finish scattering seed on six inches of snow.

Today timber cutting and grazing are in Willard's history. A mining claim still exists on the south flank of Willard Peak. Raptors, moose, deer, elk, bobcats, mountain lions, mouintain goats and bear have claimed it as their domain. Recreation is the primary use. The only new tracks etched in this soil now are those left by hikers, horseback riders, mountain bikers and all-terrain vehicles.

"It's all recreation," said Rick Vallejos, recreation specialist for the Ogden Ranger District of Wasatch-Cache National Forest. "We do have a lot of motorized recreation up there."

— Paula Huff

AUTHOR RECOMMENDATIONS

For those who like a variety of terrain and wildlife:

American Fork Twin Peaks
East Mountain
Ibapah Peak
Signal Peak

For those who prefer a long drive and a short hike:

Bluebell Knoll
South Tent Mountain
Monument Peak
Brian Head Peak

For those who want to see lots of wildflowers along the way:

Deseret Peak
Naomi Peak
Mine Camp Peak

For photographers:

Mt. Ellen
Willard Peak
Kane County's unnamed peak
Deseret Peak
Mt. Nebo North Peak
Ibapah Peak
Mt. Waas
Thurston Peak

For those in search of altitude:

Kings Peak
Gilbert Peak
Mt. Peale
Mt. Waas

For anglers (the area around the peak):

Kings Peak
Gilbert Peak
Mine Camp Peak

For those who like to route find:

Mt. Peale
Eccentric Peak
Wasatch County's high peak
East Mountain
Rich County's unnamed peak

For those who like to walk ridges:

Thurston Peak
Willard Peak
Deseret Peak
American Fork Twin Peaks
Mt. Ellen
Mt. Nebo north peak

For parents with small children who want an easy hike or for the Sunday stroller:

Kane County's high peak

For the backpacker:

Kings Peak
Gilbert Peak
Ibapah Peak
Bull Mountain

For those who like a long day hike:

Willard Peak
Mine Camp Peak
Signal Peak
Fish Lake Hightop
Ibapah Peak

For those interested in geology:

Mt. Peale
Mt. Waas
Gilbert Peak
American Fork Twin Peaks

For those who prefer hiking in wilderness areas:

Kings Peak
Gilbert Peak
Eccentric Peak
Wasatch County's unnamed peak
Mt. Nebo's north peak
Deseret Peak
Naomi Peak
Signal Peak

For those who like a well-defined, well-marked trail:

Naomi Peak
Deseret Peak

For backcountry equestrians:

Signal Peak
Mine Camp Peak
Kane County's high peak
Naomi Peak
Bull Mountain

ABOUT THE AUTHOR

Tom Wharton has been a writer at the *Salt Lake Tribune* since 1970 and in charge of the newspaper's outdoor sports coverage since 1976. During that time, he has earned many state and national writing awards from numerous professional organizations. He is currently serving as the second vice president of the Outdoor Writers Association of America. He will become president of the group in 1998.

Tom and his wife Gayen are the authors of four books with Utah themes. He graduated from the University of Utah in 1973 and served as a public affairs specialist with the Utah National Guard for 21 years.

A native Utahan, Paula Huff's early memories are of picking wild asparagus and catching frogs on the shore of a high mountain lake. She grew up loving the outdoors, and continues to do so while either hiking, back country skiing or mountain biking.

Paula graduated from Utah State University, Logan, in 1985. She works in the *Salt Lake Tribune* newspaper's Community Relations department, where she creates ads and is in charge of special projects. Hiking the highest peaks in each of Utah's counties was a series she and Tom Wharton wrote for the *Tribune's* recreation section.